What people are saying about *Handbook for*

*"If this book were available two decades ago* career would certainly have been smoother. *Ine Handbook for Early Career Success is an easy, interesting read filled with useful tips for dealing with diverse personalities. Lurie offers practical advice into managing people challenges and the conflicts that naturally occur in every workplace. While the book is a MUST read for anyone just entering the workforce, it's also a great refresher for all professionals—at any stage of life."* **Lori McDonough, VP Global Communications Prudential Financial**

*"... an excellent resource for young men and women entering the professional workforce. Lurie's approach is straight forward and easy to integrate into a workable strategy that will help mitigate mistakes that can derail a new professional career."* **Susan Greenbaum, Dean of Students, Stern School of Business Undergraduate College, New York University**

*"...a much needed practical guide that can make the difference between successfully launching a career or running into problems from the start. Lurie has made a major contribution with this text and has helped solve the problem of what to give to all soon-to-be or recent graduates."* **Ed Betof, Ed.D., Senior Fellow/Academic Director, Executive Program in Workplace Learning Leadership, The Wharton School, University of Pennsylvania**

*"...it resonated tremendously with me. It was really valuable to understand my Connecting Style, and just as valuable to understand the styles of the people I work with."* **Jeffrey Eisenberg, Advertising Programs Manager, Google**

*"...the long awaited resource that offers practical solutions for millenials and adults re-entering the most challenging work environment in many generations."* **Cecilia Holloway, Managing Director, UBS**

*"I loved this. It's excellent for early career – But great refresher for all regardless of career and years in career."* **JoAnn Ryan, CEO, Northwest Connecticut Chamber of Commerce**

*Faye,*
*Hope you enjoy this as you enter your new career in 'Philanthropy'. At least a new level. Enjoy your year of growing your career.*
*Love*

# Handbook for Early

# Career Success

*Steven Lurie, Ph.D.*

This edition published by

Dog Ear Publishing

4010 W. 86th Street, Ste H

Indianapolis, IN 46268


www.dogearpublishing.net

ISBN: **978-159858-809-5**

Library of Congress Control Number: Applied For

This book is printed on acid-free paper.


Printed in the United States of America

*To Bob Nelson — my friend, partner and mentor who taught me by example that what matters most is not which road you travel, but the difference you make to the people you meet along the way.*

# ACKNOWLEDGEMENTS

I want to express my deep appreciation to the "village" responsible for raising the *Handbook for Early Career Success* from its infancy as a half-day workshop called *School to Work* into a fully formed book. This village not only helped nurture the project to maturity, but enriched my life enormously. I want to specifically acknowledge and thank the following people for their invaluable contribution.

My experience participating in one of **Nancy Petaja's** workshops more than ten years ago left a powerful impression and helped shape both the content and approach of the *School to Work* workshop. A partner and mentor from the start in this project, her influence is reflected throughout the handbook as well. I am especially appreciative of the sections she developed – "Levels of Listening" and the "Career Entry Checklist".

When Nancy suffered a skiing accident right before our first live workshop she asked **Shelley Byan** to parachute in at the last minute (which turned into more than a year). Her incredible workshop design and facilitation instincts helped make the *School to Work* content connect powerfully to our audiences. Shelley translated her years of training young employees at JPMorgan Chase into the "Employee Etiquette" unit, a great resource for those transitioning into the workplace.

**Beth Mead** is a gifted business writer who was also on my team from the beginning. She deserves much credit for making even the most complex ideas accessible.

Through *School to Work* I became reintroduced to my cousin, **Jason Asher** (aptly named by Shelley "king of experiential learning"). His contributions as workshop facilitator and designer were, and continue to be, invaluable.

Each of my children had a hand in the workshop and handbook. **Eric**, who was actually entering the workplace from college during the piloting phase, gave us invaluable feedback about the usefulness of each component and, like **Jonny**, helped facilitate the early pilot workshops. **Briana,** while only 15 at the beginning, also pitched in with great insights and support.

Through this process I discovered that there are those special individuals who, no matter how busy they are, find the time to help. Thank you, thank you, thank you to the friends, family and colleagues who reviewed the manuscript and made it much better: **Linda Revaz, Danella Schiffer, Cathy Bergstrom, David Smith, Jeffrey Eisenberg, Michael Eisenberg, Jesse Fox, Terry Miller, Lori McDonough, Barbara Lurie, Robert DeFillippo, JoAnn Ryan, Andrew Marcus, Jeanmarie Johnson,** and **Roy Schwartz.**

Thank you to **Alison Cohen** who has assisted me and been the backbone of LED for over 15 years.

A special thanks to **Paula Schwartz,** Superintendent of Connecticut District #10 Schools, for her support and the opportunity to bring the *School to Work* workshop to the high school students and teachers in her district.

And my deep appreciation goes to **Dean Sally Lyon-Blount, Associate Dean Susan Greenbaum, Anat Lechner, Jessica Rosensweig, Jennifer Baron,** and the rest of the NYU Stern team for their sponsorship and support throughout the life of this project.

As unique as I believe the *Handbook for Early Career Success* to be, there are a number of leading thinkers in the field of Organizational Behavior who have made significant contributions that influenced the handbook: **Robert and Dorothy Bolton, Gordon Thomas, Edgar Schein, Stephen Covey** and, a mentor and friend**, Bernie Kessler** deserve special mention. Our *Connecting Style Survey* is one of many four-quadrant personality models that owe a great debt to the Social Styles concept pioneered by **David Merrill and Roger Reid** in 1964.

I want to acknowledge and thank the two mentors most influential in my professional development — **Ray Knight**, my Brandeis University psychology professor who taught me how to think like a psychologist, and **Larry Epstein**, my mentor and supervisor whose deep understanding of how people grow, succeed and find happiness serve as core principals upon which the *Handbook for Early Career Success* is based.

Finally, I want to thank my sweetheart and editor-in-chief, **Nancy Borghesi** – for her endless patience, encouragement and love.

# TABLE OF CONTENTS

# INTRODUCTION

## A Rulebook for Success

Millions of young men and women enter the workforce each year, diplomas in hand, hopes high and raring to go. The only thing they don't have is a rulebook for achieving success and happiness once they arrive. Of course, there is no such rulebook, but there are definitely rules for success. Unfortunately, most people don't discover them until well into their careers when it is too late to take advantage of them. Others never discover them and, as a result, fail to realize their potential in the workplace in spite of their talent and hard work.

The rules for career success are different from those for academic success, which may explain why the majority of college graduates, including top students from Ivy League Schools, describe themselves as failing to live up to their potential in their careers. Employer surveys confirm that young people entering the workplace are especially unprepared to meet the personal, interpersonal, and communication challenges posed by today's global workplace.

The fact that neither schools nor employers provide a roadmap for success is not a conspiracy to ensure that young people entering the workplace endure the same hardships of trial and error as those who went before them. It's just that the secrets to success lie not in any individual but in the collective experiences of people from a wide cross section of industries playing diverse roles – individuals whose careers were successful and satisfying as well as those talented individuals whose careers derailed or hit a ceiling.

Over the past 25 years, I have had the good fortune to coach hundreds of individuals representing this broad spectrum of experience. As luck would have it, New York University's Dean Sally Lyon-Blount asked me to develop a workshop to prepare NYU Stern undergraduates for a successful transition from school to work just when my own children were transitioning into the workplace. This coincidence gave me the motivation and opportunity to organize the collective wisdom of my clients, review the body of early career success research (pages 161-168), gather additional feedback from entry-level employees to industry leaders, and translate it all into this Handbook for Early Career Success.

# The High Value 21$^{st}$ Century Skills

This handbook prepares you for success in the highly interconnected global workplace where personal and interpersonal effectiveness trump the increasingly outsourced technical and analytical roles that used to be the bread and butter of the American workforce. There is little doubt this outsourcing trend will only increase in the years to come. Tom Friedman describes the implications for individual success in the ever "flattening" world of the 21$^{st}$ century: *"Those who get caught in the past and resist change will be forced deeper into commoditization. Those who can create value through leadership, relationship and creativity will transform the industry as well as strengthen relationships with their existing clients...No matter what your profession – doctor, lawyer architect, accountant – if you are an American, you had better be good at the touchy feely service stuff because anything that can be digitized can be outsourced to either the smartest or the cheapest producer or both...everyone has to focus on exactly what is their value added."*[1]

Ironically, almost all the value you will be asked to add during the first years in the workplace fits into the category of easily outsourced "low-value" or commoditized work. Not to worry. Excelling in the technical and analytical roles is how you earn your stripes, cut your teeth, or get your sea legs – take your pick. This handbook accelerates your development of those high value personal and interpersonal skills – skills that will not only distinguish your early career performance, but also lay the foundation for a successful, satisfying and self-directed career.

# The Layout of the Handbook

*The handbook is organized into the following four parts:*

## Part One: Connecting for Success

Perhaps the most profound difference between school and work is that in school you are a "me," whereas in the workplace you are contributing as part of and through an interconnected and global "we" (Unit 1). Starting with your first days on the job, people you think don't even know you exist will form strong first impressions based on everything you do or say. These *First Impressions* (Unit 2), subjective as they are, can dramatically influence your future.

Making a strong first impression is much more likely if you understand the *Six Basic Connecting Needs* (Unit 3). This must-read unit teaches you the natural laws of connection and lays out the specific behaviors that will make the difference between engaging openness and cooperation versus defensiveness and competition.

No matter how well you know the behavioral rules for connecting, if you don't know how you come across or that you have big blind spots (Unit 4), you cannot effectively influence how others will react to you.

## Part Two: Connecting Style

Units 5-8 focus on understanding your *Connecting Style*, and help you develop a much clearer and realistic sense of who you are as others see you. By following the directions for the easily self-administered *Connecting Style Survey*, you will find out which of four *Connecting Styles* best describes you. This section provides a wealth of information about all four styles and provides invaluable insights about yourself and others, including who you are as others see you, the situations that bring out the best in you, the team roles to which you gravitate, your blind spots and much more. <u>To get the most from this handbook, it is highly recommended that you complete the survey before proceeding to the sections that follow it.</u>

*Connecting Across Styles* and *Guidelines for Connecting with Each Style* (Units 9 and 10) provide guidance for building relationships with the 75 percent of the world whose styles are different from yours.

*Increasing Role Versatility* (Unit 11) takes you through an exercise to sharpen your awareness of the roles in which you feel least comfortable and will help you develop a strategy to make you more effective in those roles.

Unit 12 provides specific instructions for *Assessing Connecting Style in Others* and an exercise to test your Connecting Style assessment skills.

Unit 13 illustrates how to apply the *Six Basic Connecting Needs* awareness to significantly enhance interpersonal effectiveness at work.

## *Part Three: 21ˢᵗ Century Self-Empowerment Skills*

*Listening* (Unit 14), *Self-Directed Learning* (Unit 15), *Self-Discipline* (Unit 16), *Habit Change* (Unit 17), *Networking* (Unit 18) and *Stress Resilience* (Unit 19) are among the most important competencies for thriving in the global workplace, yet least likely to be learned in school. These skills will help to empower you from your first to your last day in the workplace. Whether you are an intern or managing partner, a trainee or CEO, these six skill sets are the secret to a self-directed path to success. While essential to early career success, they are also among the most underdeveloped skills. So paying careful attention to these units will yield an excellent "return on your investment."

## *Part Four: Rules of the Road*

*Eight Keys to Early Career Success* (Unit 20) describes in detail the qualities that lead to early career success and how you can achieve them.

*Workplace Etiquette* (Unit 21) provides specific behavioral guidance and standards of etiquette for everyday activities and challenges that you will not have faced much in school. This section represents the consensus of the very people who will be evaluating your performance. If you want to understand the secrets of those who differentiate themselves as *great rather than just good performers*, read this section carefully.

Unit 22, *Career Entry Checklist* is designed to help assure an organized and smooth entry to a new job.

*Common Career Derailers* (Unit 23) describes some of the more common career damaging behaviors responsible for stalling or ruining many a promising career, and the *Career Risk Factor Self-Assessment* (Unit 24) is a brief survey you can complete to assess your own career vulnerabilities.

The *Appendix* contains a summary of recent early career success research and references to important books, websites and other resources.

Finally, exercises can be found throughout the book immediately following this symbol.

These exercises are designed to help you connect the information, insights and advice to your own personal experience and development. The *Appendix* also contains *Development Planning Forms* to help you achieve the development goals you set based on these exercises.

Congratulations! The discipline and curiosity required to have read to this point in the book are qualities that will help you thrive in a competitive workplace. I wrote this handbook with you in mind.

I hope you enjoy it.

Best wishes for a successful and satisfying career.

Steven Lurie, Ph.D.
January 26, 2009

# BEFORE YOU GET OUT OF THE GATE

Unlike school, where the emphasis was on learning the 'what,' 'why,' and 'how' of the world, this handbook starts with a focus on the 'who' – as in you. Throughout your career, you are likely to feel pressured by family and peers to take 'the path most traveled.' The more self-aware you are, the more likely you will be able to find and take the path that is best for you.

Never underestimate yourself and the things you can accomplish. I am sure that many of you have already set your goals based on what is realistic and safe, rather than following your dreams. If you have any doubts about whether you can achieve *any* goal you can imagine, consider the power of your pedigree:

"Consider the fact that for 3.8 billion years – a period of time older than the earth's mountains and rivers and oceans – every one of your forbearers on both sides has been attractive enough to find a mate, healthy enough to reproduce and sufficiently blessed by fate and circumstances to live long enough to do so. Not one of your pertinent ancestors was squashed, devoured, drowned, starved, stuck fast, untimely injured, or otherwise deflected from its life's quest to deliver a tiny charge of genetic material to the right partner at the right moment in order to perpetuate the only combination of genetic materials that could result, eventually astoundingly, and all too briefly in you." (Bill Bryson. *A Short History of Nearly Everything*. [New York: Broadway Books, 2003]).

So with 3.8 billion years of ancestral success behind you, how can you fail?

PART ONE

# Connecting for Success

# Unit 1.
# From Me to We

The successful transition from school to work starts with the recognition of the fundamental differences between these two worlds.

| AT SCHOOL... | AT WORK... |
| --- | --- |
| You pay them, so you are the customer. | They pay you, so everyone else (your boss, the organization, and all its stakeholders) is your customer. |
| Your goal is to demonstrate your knowledge and proficiency as an individual. | Your goal is to add value by applying your knowledge and proficiency as part of an interconnected social system. |
| Leveraging the talent and experience of your colleagues is considered 'cheating' and gets you in trouble. | Leveraging the talent and experience of your colleagues is considered 'collaborating' and leads to success. |
| Your role, responsibilities, and performance standards are well defined. | Your role, responsibilities, and performance standards can be ambiguous and fluid. Your job is largely what you make it. |
| Your success is based purely on the quality of your work product. | The impressions you make are key to success! |

The last difference in our table between school and work represents an early stumbling block for many new employees. So, let us start with first impressions.

# UNIT 2.
# FIRST IMPRESSIONS

The first day you report for your first job, you have no history, no baggage. One of the things that make it so exciting is that you get to start with a blank page. At the same time, you have no track record at the very point in time that people will be scrutinizing you most. What they see and hear in your first few days becomes the basis of their opinions about you. These superficial impressions will factor into what decision makers think of you, and will lay the groundwork for your future.

Forming impressions is not about manipulating public opinion about you so much as making sure that the perceptions others have are *accurate* and reflect your strongest assets and abilities.

Imagine yourself in an orientation meeting with a group of other new hires listening to a manager describe the health benefits package. You'll probably have more than a few such orientation meetings during your first weeks on the job. Although the experience might make you feel anonymous, surprisingly, you are already shaping the manager's impressions about you.

Right or wrong, any manager who has spent 15 minutes presenting to new employees already has good feelings about some and negative feelings about others based on dozens of invisible interactions.

Imagine someone yawning or slouching while the manager explains company health benefits, while another person leans forward, makes eye contact, and nods to register understanding, and yet another new hire takes notes or perhaps asks a question. Your body language and the attitudes it conveys in a college classroom may be noticeable to the instructor, but inconsequential. In the workplace, non-verbal communication can have a powerful impact, stimulating either negative or positive emotional reactions in everyone around you. Over time, the overall pattern of engaging versus distancing behaviors creates enduring impressions.

The point is that the "product" is you and the good news is that we understand a great deal about the behaviors that will generate good feelings about you, and more importantly, about those that will lead people to trust you and want to work with you. The key is the extent to which others perceive your behavior as supporting or frustrating the six universal human needs. I call them the *Six Basic Connecting Needs*.

1. Ask three to five friends or colleagues to share their first impressions of you. If possible, ask them to write or email them. This approach tends to provide richer and more thoughtful responses.
2. Based on all of the impressions, what patterns emerged? What surprised you most?

_____
_____
_____
_____
_____
_____
_____
_____
_____
_____
_____
_____
_____
_____
_____
_____
_____
_____
_____
_____
_____
_____
_____
_____
_____
_____
_____

# UNIT 3.
# SIX BASIC CONNECTING NEEDS

**How do I connect with others in a way that leads them...**

- to be comfortable working with me?
- to trust in and rely upon me?
- to be open to my ideas?
- to include me in important decisions?
- to give me the benefit of the doubt?
- to choose me for the key roles and jobs?

**How do I keep coworkers from being...**

- resistant or defensive?
- discounting or dismissing my contribution?
- misunderstanding my good intentions?

How receptive or defensive other people are toward you is based largely upon:

- Your ability to communicate in the style most comfortable for the receiver – we call this *Connecting Style* and will address this in detail in the next section.
- The extent to which your behavior supports or frustrates the following *Six Basic Connecting Needs* in the people with whom you are interacting. These are the need to feel:

1.  Basic Trust

2.  Understood

3.  Valued

4.  Included

5.  Respected

6.  Autonomous (in control).

When your behavior supports these needs in others, you will create a receptive and supportive audience. Conversely, violation of one or more of these needs causes almost all defensive and antagonistic reactions. Once you identify the specific need or needs that have been frustrated, you can take action to support them and rebuild trust. A description of these six needs follows. Although each need is different, you will notice that they overlap one another. Pay close attention to the behaviors that support or frustrate each need.

## *Supporting the Six Basic Connecting Needs*

| The other person needs to feel: | You support their need by: | You frustrate their need by: |
| --- | --- | --- |
| **Basic Trust**<br>I trust that you are who you say you are. I don't have to watch my back. Your behavior reflects integrity, candor and high moral and ethical standards. I feel secure in knowing that you are sincere, have good intentions, and my best interests at heart. | ☐ Being sincere and genuine<br>☐ Keeping confidential discussions confidential<br>☐ Being dependable; delivering on promises; following up on commitments; being on time<br>☐ Showing you have the courage of your convictions, and standing up for your beliefs, even if they are unpopular<br>☐ Taking responsibility for mistakes<br>☐ Demonstrating loyalty<br>☐ Expressing disagreements directly rather than being a 'yes' person | ☐ Having hidden agendas<br>☐ Telling half-truths or embellishing<br>☐ Sharing confidential information or taking part in gossip<br>☐ Covering up mistakes<br>☐ Blaming others<br>☐ Taking credit for other's work<br>☐ 'Working the system' or taking inappropriate advantage of policy |
| **Understood**<br>You get me! You understand what I am saying, how I feel about it, and what it means to me. | ☐ Listening<br>☐ Demonstrating interest in learning what it is like to be in the other person's shoes<br>☐ Restating what you hear<br>☐ Asking good questions | ☐ Assuming you already understand<br>☐ Seeking to be understood before demonstrating that you understand<br>☐ Prematurely prescribing solutions<br>☐ Arguing or disagreeing without fully understanding what the other person is saying<br>☐ Using body language that signals you are not listening |

| The other person needs to feel: | You support their need by: | You frustrate their need by: |
|---|---|---|
| **Valued**<br>I am appreciated for what I do and who I am. I am perceived as making a difference, adding value, and contributing to something important. | ☐ Finding merit in what others say and do<br>☐ Thanking people in person or through 'thank you' notes or voicemail messages<br>☐ Expressing appreciation for how you or others have benefited from something the other person said or did<br>☐ Asking for advice or help | ☐ Criticizing<br>☐ One-upping<br>☐ Discounting or dismissing<br>☐ Prescribing solutions or solving other's problem directly before they ask<br>☐ Bragging |
| **Included**<br>I belong. I am invited into the inner circle. I feel like one of the gang, a vital part of the community or team. | ☐ Asking other's opinion<br>☐ Consulting with others<br>☐ Asking others to join committees<br>☐ Using others as a sounding board<br>☐ Sharing something personal<br>☐ Inviting others (to meetings, lunch, etc.) | ☐ Excluding others<br>☐ Making decisions without input from others<br>☐ Keeping to yourself<br>☐ Having sidebar conversations in group gatherings |
| **Respected**<br>I am treated in a way that acknowledges and recognizes my status, experience, knowledge, territory, authority, values, traditions, customs, and preferences, whether I am a mailroom clerk or CEO! | ☐ Demonstrating that you have paid close attention to what is important to the other person<br>☐ Listening<br>☐ Apologizing once you realize you have 'stepped on someone's toes'<br>☐ Taking other people's needs seriously, but not taking yourself seriously – modesty and self-deprecating humor go a long way | ☐ Not taking the time to understand what is important to others<br>☐ Being sarcastic or using humor to put others down<br>☐ Condescending, critical, or dismissive behavior |

17

| The other person needs to feel: | You support their need by: | You frustrate their need by: |
|---|---|---|
| **Respected** (cont'd) | ☐ Understanding how the other person sees their role, priorities, and hot button issues<br>☐ Recognizing their accomplishments<br>☐ Demonstrating appreciation<br>☐ Supporting the other person's position, power, and status the way they define it<br>☐ Working through traditional channels and chain of command<br>☐ Asking for help, expertise, and consultation | ☐ Violating role boundaries, chain of command, or tradition<br>☐ Inflating your contribution and minimizing or ignoring the contribution made by others<br>☐ Coming across as a missionary on a quest to civilize and convert ("Let me tell you how we did it at ABC Company…"), rather than as an anthropologist trying to learn and understand |
| **Autonomous**<br>I feel free to make my own decisions and not have someone else's decisions imposed on me. I feel I run my own life. I am treated democratically rather than dictatorially. I have ownership for my work and its outcome. | ☐ Asking for permission to enter their space, "Do you mind if I ask a question…make a suggestion…interrupt for a moment…give you some feedback..?"<br>☐ Allowing others to figure things out for themselves and arrive at their own solutions<br>☐ Giving choices<br>☐ Using a participative leadership style | ☐ Forcing unwanted opinions or advice on others<br>☐ Telling others what to do<br>☐ Keeping others out of decision-making loop<br>☐ 'Rescuing' others when they haven't asked for your help |

18

Notice there are some behaviors, like listening and finding merit, that support almost all of these universal needs. These become everyday habits for effective relationship building. These habits include:

- behaving with modesty and humility
- treating people with respect and acceptance and never talking down to them
- being polite
- listening, listening, listening and demonstrating that you understand more than just the message, but its context and the emotions behind it too
- communicating in a style that fits the listener's comfort zone, not yours
- taking the time to understand and show respect for the needs, preferences, style, values, and accomplishments of the people with whom you work
- demonstrating appreciation through finding merit: giving credit, skillful praise and thanks for good work, and avoiding criticism
- going out of your way to be supportive (and keeping critical feelings about others to yourself)
- including others through getting their advice and sharing your ideas, opinions, and feelings
- following up on promises
- being sincere
- accepting responsibility for your own mistakes and decisions
- apologizing when you have offended someone

Remember, you get back from others exactly what you give!

1. Review all of the behaviors in second and third columns on pages 16-18 and in the box on the left of each item, place a checkmark next to any behavior that you believe you can improve on in your day-to-day interactions.
2. Go back and select the three behaviors that you feel will be most important for you to address during the next few months.
3. Following the instructions on page 151, create a development plan for each of those behaviors. Use the forms on pages 153-160.

# UNIT 4.
# THE BLIND SPOT

"They almost always report feeling blindsided when
they hit that ceiling and discover the gap between their
positive intentions and their actual negative impact of their
behavior on others."

Barbara Kovach, *Organizational Dynamics*, 1986 (Describing young men and women who
derail from the fast track in mid-career).

Unfortunately, we're not always aware of when we are
supporting or frustrating the Six Basic Connecting Needs.

Most often, it is the behaviors we are not aware of that have the
greatest impact on how people feel about us. These are largely non-
verbal behaviors such as facial expression, tone of voice, or eye
contact.. In other words, most of the things that people do to irritate
each other are in a BLIND SPOT.

Just as we are partially blind to the negative impact we can have
on others, most of us are largely unaware of what we do that makes
us valued and appreciated. I don't think I really understood this until
I was nearly 15 years into my management consulting career.

The general counsel of a major entertainment company asked me
to lunch to discuss a serious personnel issue in his department. This
very senior executive was not only a very important client, but the
organizational decisions he made had important consequences to
many individuals across a number of entertainment divisions and I
was quite conscious of wanting to provide the best counsel possible.

The restaurant he chose happened to be very crowded and with
its very high ceilings I found myself straining to hear as he was
telling me the details of his challenge. I said "excuse me would you
repeat that. I couldn't hear what you were saying." After about ten
minutes of "sorry", "say again", and "pardon me's" I resigned myself
to the fact that we would have to continue the discussion after lunch
or reschedule. As we were leaving the restaurant I was about to
suggest we reschedule when he turned to me to thank me for being
so helpful. He was uncharacteristically appreciative of my

consultation and felt very good about the solution that came out of our "discussion."

Good thing I couldn't hear well enough to analyze the issues and provide him sage advice. Through no fault of my own, I gave him what he really needed – the opportunity to talk through his problem with someone who was strenuously listening to his every word while providing him the space to formulate his own solution. Through that accident, I became aware of how much I had been overrating the importance of advice-giving, as the key to being helpful and underrating the power of listening, especially when working with very self-reliant and competent people.

It's hard to know when we are overusing the behaviors that come most naturally to us. I recently sat in on a meeting held by a rather forceful but well-meaning senior executive to pump up and empower a new team he inherited. He wanted to let them know how important their feedback was to him and how open he was to hearing it. He spent about 20 minutes telling story after story about how feedback helped him over the years, but then ran out of time before anyone else had the chance to speak. His mixed message reflected a big blind spot – that listening, valuing and including his new team meant much more to them than explaining, teaching and lecturing them — what he most enjoyed doing.

Finally, a very nurturing but conflict averse young employee was sharing how worried she was about what people at work would think of her after she finally insisted that two people who were constantly fooling around during meetings, stop! She was concerned that "they are going to think I am a real bitch". The reality was that the other people at the meeting nearly applauded because they were so pleased to see her asserting herself.

These vignettes illustrate another important point about blind spots. Most of the time, the strengths we are least aware of are qualities that are typical of styles totally opposite from our own. More forcefully assertive people overestimate their value as driver of results or solver of problem and underestimate the power of listening and being supportive. More quietly assertive people underestimate the positive impact of forceful behavior.

Just as our car's blind spot is blamed for so many automobile crashes, so too is the human blind spot responsible for so many of our career crashes. But like we learned in driver's education, once you know about the blind spot, you are responsible for doing the hard work of turning your head around to look before changing lanes or pulling out of your parking spot. Once you look at the area that your mirror cannot see, it is no longer a blind spot. And forgiving this extended analogy, our behavioral blind spot will be trouble for us only to the extent that we don't bother to get feedback from others about who we are as others see us and observing people's reactions to our behavior in the moment.

Understanding what is in your blind spot is a lifelong process, so why not start now.

The following units on Connecting Style will provide invaluable information about your blind spots and the impact, both positive and negative, that you are likely to have on others.

1. Identify three people who know you well, but each in a different context, that you can ask for feedback about your blind spot.

2. Prior to getting their feedback, write down what you think they might say.

_____
_____
_____
_____
_____
_____
_____
_____
_____
_____

3.  Ask them to share with you what they think are your blind spots including strengths and weaknesses. Make sure they know that this is an important part of your professional development and that you want to apply their feedback to improve your effectiveness. If they seem to be having trouble understanding what you are looking for, give them a copy of this unit to read.

4.  Write down their comments and refer to them after you have had the chance to complete the Connecting Style Survey in Unit 6 and compare their feedback with the strengths and weaknesses characteristics of your style.

_____

_____

_____

_____

_____

_____

_____

_____

_____

_____

_____

_____

_____

_____

_____

_____

_____

_____

PART TWO

# Connecting Style

# Unit 5.
# Introducing Connecting Style

So what exactly do I mean by *"Connecting Style"*? Imagine if someone asked 100 people who have known you well — each during a different period of your life and in different settings — to pick five words or phrases that best describe you. The same words would come up over and over again forming a pattern or consensus of how people experience you. Moreover, if you compared the words most commonly used to describe you with those most commonly used to describe any group of people picked at random; you would find that the words used to describe about one-quarter of all people are *remarkably similar* to the ones used to describe you. Words that are strikingly *different* than those used to describe you would apply to another quarter. The other half of the group would be described with words some of which you share in common and some of which you do not.

I call these patterns of behavior *'Connecting Style'* – the consensus of the impressions you make and the impact you have on others based on everything you do and say, knowingly and unknowingly, across different situations over the course of your life. Every one of us has a unique personality. Yet it is also the case that we divide naturally into one of four broad but distinct behavioral styles. Furthermore, people that share the same style have remarkable similarities in how they approach problems, the roles they prefer when working in teams, how they communicate, build relationships, respond to threat, conflict and stress. They even seem to agree about the kinds of people they click with and the habits and behaviors they find most irritating. So understanding someone's style allows you to tune in to their needs, preferences and reactions, making it much easier to connect with them. Add to that an awareness of how their style interacts with your style, and you have a foundation for successful communicating and relationship building in all of life's interactions, in and out of the workplace.

Starting in 1964 with the "social styles personality model" developed by David Merrill and Roger Reid, at least a dozen four-style preference personality models have been developed and used extensively in the workplace, each with their unique strengths and limitations. The *Connecting Style* model I developed for our workshops and this handbook takes what I believe are the best features of each of these models and integrates them with behavioral dimensions I discovered to be most relevant to success in today's world. The result is the *Connecting Style Survey*, a simple yet powerful tool with a number of important advantages borne out by feedback collected from readers and workshop participants over the past several years:

1. Unlike other surveys, the *Connecting Style Survey* is quickly and easily self-administered and scored, and quite accurate.

2. In minutes, people learn how to use behavioral observation to assess the *Connecting Styles* of others – even those they just met.

3. The *Connecting Style* model helps people predict and thereby prepare for the sudden and often counterproductive behavior changes brought on by stress.

4. The language, style descriptions, insights and style-related recommendations are non-threatening, easily grasped, yet powerful and compelling. The insights are readily applied both in and out of the workplace.

5. The insights gleaned from the Connecting Style Survey and tools are applicable to the development of people as individuals, workgroups and organizations.

6. It has applications for improving relationship building, communications, influencing and leadership effectiveness.

7. The tool resonates powerfully with audiences from 14 to 80, from people on the loading dock to those in corner offices.

What you should know about the *Connecting Style Survey* to ensure that you get the most from it:

People fall into one of four *Connecting Styles* based on two aspects of their observable behavior – how emotionally they connect (emotional responsiveness) and how forcefully verses quietly they connect (assertiveness). More about these qualities on the next page.

- The purpose of the *Connecting Style Survey* is not to place you and others in a box. Everyone behaves in ways that reflect qualities of all four styles on a regular basis. Your *Connecting Style* reflects a pattern of behavior that is simply most automatic and natural. By increasing behavioral awareness, the *Connecting Style Survey* actually helps people expand outside of their boxes and leads to style flexibility – the key to success.

- Each *Connecting Style* has characteristic strengths and limitations. No one style is "better" than any other. Great parents, teachers, artists, executives, scientists, chefs, politicians, etc. come in all styles. But for each style there is a slightly different path to success.

- *Connecting Style* is not in any way predictive of what are perhaps the important human qualities like courage, honesty, loyalty, integrity, compassion, and discipline.

Now let's take closer look at the two dimensions of connecting that determine one's *Connecting Style*.

# Emotional Responsiveness and Assertiveness

1. <u>Emotional Responsiveness</u> refers to the degree to which a person responds to and expresses emotions in behaviorally observable ways. Some are less emotionally responsive or *Task-Oriented* and others are more emotionally responsive or *Relationship-Oriented*.

2. <u>Assertiveness</u> refers to how *quietly* or *forcefully* a person connects.

Before completing the *Connecting Style Survey* form on page 35, review the behavioral qualities on the following page that determine whether you would be considered more *Relationship* or *Task Oriented*, and more *Quietly* or *Forcefully Assertive*.

| Task Oriented (Less Emotionally Responsive) | Relationship Oriented (More Emotionally Responsive) |
|---|---|
| 1. Information focused | 1. People focused |
| 2. Attuned to facts | 2. Attuned to feelings |
| 3. Less use of expressive gestures | 3. Greater use of expressive gestures |
| 4. More limited facial animation | 4. More facial animation |
| 5. Little voice variation | 5. More voice variation |
| 6. Contain feelings | 6. Express feelings |
| 7. More serious and formal | 7. More playful and relaxed |

| Quietly Assertive | Forcefully Assertive |
|---|---|
| 1. Ask | 1. Tell |
| 2. Listen / reflect | 2. Talk / act |
| 3. Move less and slower | 3. Move more and faster |
| 4. Talk less, softer and slower | 4. Talk more, louder and faster |
| 5. Lean back | 5. Lean forward |
| 6. Less confrontational | 6. More confrontational |
| 7. Decide less quickly | 7. Decide more quickly |

# UNIT 6.
## SELF-SCORING THE CONNECTING STYLE SURVEY

Please refer to the *Connecting Style Survey Self-Scoring Form Illustration* on page 34 as you read through these instructions.

**1. Determine the answer to the question: "Is my style more *Task Oriented* or *Relationship Oriented* and how pronounced is the difference?"** Under *Task Oriented* and *Relationship Oriented* are seven pairs of behavioral descriptors. For each of the seven pairs of descriptors, select the one that best describes you by checking the box next to the item. For example, referring to the first pair of descriptors in the illustration, Nancy perceives herself to be more naturally "people-focused" than "information-focused" so she checked the box next to "people-focused."

**The most common question is: "What do I do if I act differently depending on where I am and who I am with?" For example, when I am at work, I am more 'information-focused'. With my friends, I am more 'people-focused'.** The answer: Choose the behavior that feels most natural. If you are still unsure, ask yourself which choice the majority of the 100 people who know you best would recommend.

Nancy went on to check the box next to all seven descriptors under *Relationship Oriented*. So Nancy would be considered more *Relationship Oriented* because she chose more *Relationship Oriented* descriptors than *Task Oriented* descriptors. Nancy then placed an **X** in the box with the number 7 in it, since that is how many *Relationship Oriented* items she checked.

Now, before proceeding to item 2 below, go to page 35, *Connecting Style Survey Self-Scoring Form*, and select one item from each of the seven pairs under *Relationship Oriented* and *Task Oriented* by checking off the appropriate boxes. Then place an **X** in the box with the number that coincides with the total number of items checked under either *Task Oriented* or *Relationship Oriented*, whichever is the higher number (just as Nancy did).

**2. Next, determine the answer to the question: "Is my style more *Quietly Assertive* or *Forcefully Assertive* and how pronounced is the difference?"** Follow the same instructions as you did in (1) above. Looking at the illustrations, Nancy selected five items under *Forcefully Assertive* and only two under *Quietly Assertive,* so she put an **X** in the box marked "5" located on the right or *Forcefully Assertive* side of the vertical line.

Now go to page 35, *Connecting Style Survey Self-Scoring Form*, and select one item from each of the seven pairs under *Quietly Assertive* and *Forcefully Assertive* by checking off the appropriate boxes, and place an **X** in the box with the number that coincides with the total number of items checked under either *Quietly Assertive* or *Forcefully Assertive*, whichever is the higher number (just as Nancy did). Then draw an intersecting line to connect the two **X**'s as illustrated and mark that point of intersection with an **X**, just as Nancy did.

**NAME: Nancy**

## Connecting Style Survey Scoring Form Illustration

### Task Oriented (less Emotionally Responsive)

☐ 1. Information focused
☐ 2. Attuned to facts
☐ 3. Less use of expressive gestures
☐ 4. More limited facial animation
☐ 5. Little voice variation
☐ 6. Contain feelings
☐ 7 More serious and formal

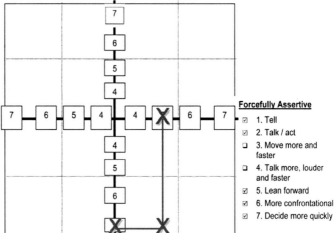

**Quietly Assertive**

☐ 1. Ask
☐ 2. Listen / reflect
☑ 3. Move less and slower
☑ 4. Talk less, softer and slower
☐ 5. Lean back
☐ 6. Less confrontational
☐ 7. Decide less quickly

**Forcefully Assertive**

☑ 1. Tell
☑ 2. Talk / act
☐ 3. Move more and faster
☐ 4. Talk more, louder and faster
☑ 5. Lean forward
☑ 6. More confrontational
☑ 7. Decide more quickly

### Relationship Oriented (more Emotionally Responsive

☑ 1. People focused
☑ 2 .Attuned to feelings
☑ 3. Greater use of expressive gestures
☑ 4. More facial animation
☑ 5. More voice variation
☑ 6. Express feelings
☑ 7. More playful and relaxed

## Connecting Style Survey Self-Scoring Form

### Task Oriented (Less Emotionally Responsive)

- ❏ 1 .Information focused
- ❏ 2. Attuned to facts
- ❏ 3. Less use of expressive gestures
- ❏ 4. More limited facial animation
- ❏ 5. Little voice variation
- ❏ 6. Contain feelings
- ❏ 7. More serious and formal

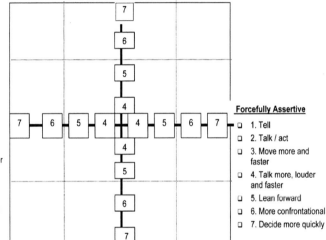

**Quietly Assertive**

- ❏ 1. Ask
- ❏ 2. Listen / reflect
- ❏ 3. Move less and slower
- ❏ 4. Talk less, softer and slower
- ❏ 5. Lean back
- ❏ 6. Less confrontational
- ❏ 7 .Decide less quickly

**Forcefully Assertive**

- ❏ 1. Tell
- ❏ 2. Talk / act
- ❏ 3. Move more and faster
- ❏ 4. Talk more, louder and faster
- ❏ 5. Lean forward
- ❏ 6. More confrontational
- ❏ 7. Decide more quickly

### Relationship Oriented (More Emotionally Responsive)

- ❏ 1. People focused
- ❏ 2. Attuned to feelings
- ❏ 3. Greater use of expressive gestures
- ❏ 4. More facial animation
- ❏ 5. More voice variation
- ❏ 6. Express feelings
- ❏ 7. More playful and relaxed

35

## The Names of the Four Style Quadrants

Each of these quadrants represents a style. Write them in on the *Connecting Style Self-Scoring* grid as I describe each one.

The quadrant in the top left is called **Analytical** – people in this quadrant are more *quietly assertive* and *task oriented*; the role most natural for them in a team setting is critical thinker.

Moving to the right, people who fall in the next quadrant are more *task oriented* like the **Analytical**, but are more *forcefully assertive*. These people are referred to as **Drivers** and are comfortable in the director role.

Continuing clockwise, people who fall into the next quadrant are more *forcefully assertive* like **Drivers**, but are more *relationship oriented*. These folks are referred to as **Energizers** – and the role they like to play is team builder. Notice that **Energizers** and **Analyticals** share neither of the two personality attributes.

Like **Energizers**, people in this next quadrant are more *relationship oriented*, but like **Analyticals**, they are more *quietly assertive*. Those who fit in this quadrant are **Supportives** – they are *relationship oriented* and *quietly assertive* and commonly play the role of team player.

Which style has no personality traits in common with **Supportive**? If you guessed **Driver**, you guessed correctly!

# UNIT 7.
## SECONDARY STYLE

Now transpose the **X** that you marked in your quadrant onto the exact same place on the grid on the following page. Notice that you fall in a sub-quadrant or secondary style within your style quadrant <u>depending on how pronounced your behavior is</u> in each of the two personality dimensions. If a **Driver's** task orientation is pronounced (let's say she circled seven items under *task oriented*), but she is only slightly more forcefully assertive than quietly assertive (let's say she circled four items under *forcefully assertive* and three under *quietly assertive*), she would fall into the **Analytical** sub-quadrant within the **Driver** quadrant. This suggests that she would be almost as comfortable describing herself as an **Analytical** as she would a **Driver**. In a group of **Drivers**, she would gravitate toward the critical thinker role of an **Analytical**.

Which secondary style would an **Energizer** have who is extremely assertive but only slightly more relationship oriented? If you answered **Driver**, you are correct. That individual will seem like a **Driver** in a group of fellow **Energizers**.

In which sub-quadrant would an **Energizer** fall who is forcefully assertive and far more relationship oriented than task oriented? Their secondary style would be the same as their primary style. In other words, they are extreme **Energizers**.

# Primary and Secondary Styles

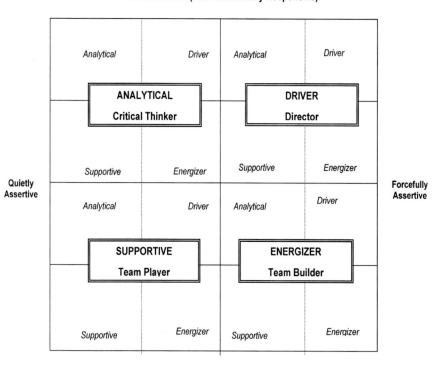

Task Oriented (Less Emotionally Responsive)

Relationship Oriented (More Emotionally Responsive)

# The Four Connecting Styles – Common Characteristics

To make sure you are in the quadrant that best describes you, please refer to the column below that represents your style as scored. Review the descriptions underneath your style name to make sure that they describe you more accurately than the descriptions under the other three styles. It is not uncommon for some to discover that the style from the previous exercise does not capture him or her as well as another style. If this is the case for you, think of yourself as the style that best describes you below, rather than how you scored yourself in the survey.

| Analytical "Critical Thinker" | Driver "Director" | Energizer "Team Builder" | Supportive "Team Player" |
|---|---|---|---|
| ☐ Logical<br>☐ Data driven<br>☐ Precise<br>☐ Emotionally controlled<br>☐ Quietly determined, focused<br>☐ Patient with complex challenges<br>☐ Serious<br>☐ Private<br>☐ Methodical<br>☐ Cautious decision maker | ☐ Strong willed<br>☐ Results driven<br>☐ Not easily influenced<br>☐ Takes charge quickly<br>☐ Action oriented<br>☐ Direct and to-the-point<br>☐ Independent<br>☐ Decisive<br>☐ Practical<br>☐ Impatient | ☐ Social<br>☐ Expresses lots of ideas<br>☐ Loves fun and spontaneity<br>☐ Stimulating<br>☐ Promoter<br>☐ Enthusiastic<br>☐ Seeks approval<br>☐ Jumps from one activity to another<br>☐ Bored with details<br>☐ Inconsistent follow through | ☐ Accommodating<br>☐ Good listener<br>☐ Open and sharing<br>☐ Modest<br>☐ Implementer<br>☐ Patient<br>☐ Service oriented<br>☐ Likes structured, stable settings<br>☐ Cautious<br>☐ Dependable<br>☐ Pliable<br>☐ Willing |

Ask 3-5 people to review the common characteristics of each of the four styles above and rank them from 1 (most like you) to 4 (least like you). Where differences exist, review them with the raters.

# UNIT 8.
## CONNECTING STYLE AND TIPS

The following eight pages contain descriptions of each Connecting Style and tips for connecting more effectively.

1.  Read the two pages associated with your primary style and the two pages associated with your secondary style. On the pages titled *Connecting Style Description*, highlight those areas that resonate most with you. On the *Tips* pages, highlight the ones that best reflect the behavioral changes you want to make.

2.  Select two to four of the behavioral changes you highlighted and using the *Development Plan Forms* in the Appendix, create a development plan for each.

3.  Don't forget to read the pages describing the other two connecting styles.

## *Analyticals / Critical Thinkers*
# Connecting Style Description

The most controlled and private of the four styles, **Analyticals** are the hardest to read and get to know. Like everyone else, they have strong passions, opinions and emotions, but since they are often uncomfortable sharing them, they risk being misread or misunderstood as cold, detached, or lacking enthusiasm.

Their focus on tasks, facts, and ideas is at the forefront of their working style. They spend much of their time gathering and analyzing data – asking a lot of questions about specific details. They appreciate structure and organization and take a systematic, detailed approach to communicating. The detailed approach and sometimes slow pace of the **Analytical** can be frustrating to the **Driver** and **Energizer** who may tune out or want to jump in to help move the **Analyticals** to act.

Of the four styles, **Analyticals** can be the most critical; hard on both themselves and others. They make excellent critical thinkers, often acting as the protector of data integrity on a team, but as they focus on solving the problem, they can appear to be critical of others. Their opinions carry weight as they are well articulated and supported by lots of evidence. Finding merit and expressing appreciation does not come naturally to them, so when they do express appreciation or praise, it has a powerful effect.

## *Analyticals / Critical Thinkers*

## Tips

❑ Express appreciation – find merit in others' words and actions; let people know how they have had a positive impact (e.g., "you got me thinking"; "our discussion came in handy"; "I quoted you the other day").

❑ When you disagree, find a positive and valuing way to express it. Disagree only after you demonstrate that you find merit in some aspect of their point.

❑ Share more of what you are thinking and feeling.

❑ Share something personal – especially with Supportives and Energizers.

❑ Demonstrate more enthusiasm when working with others or listening to others – nod your head, smile, and use more inflection in your voice.

❑ Move more quickly and speak faster than you normally do. Act with enthusiasm!

❑ Reduce the amount of facts and figures in your conversations. Be more casual!

❑ Be aware of the body language of others – adjust your communication in reaction to their movement.

❑ Spice up or shorten your delivery as you see your audience fading.

## *Drivers / Directors*
## Connecting Style Description

**Drivers** are very strong communicators who are excellent at expressing their opinions. Their certainty and organized thinking makes them compelling, and their direct to-the-point style adds to their credibility. They get people's attention and gain their confidence. *"She really knows what she is talking about."*

But their desire for results often leads Drivers to rush to conclusions without properly vetting their assumptions or verifying facts. In the pressure of the workplace, when they see a solution, their inclination is to get it done rather than ask questions (Is it the best solution? What have I missed? Do I have all the facts?). Their natural independence and confidence causes them to inadvertently exclude others from their decision-making process. Drivers often ask for input after they've already committed to their own ideas. At that point, input from others is marginalized.

**Drivers** are often surprised that others find them intimidating and defensive. They do not recognize the impatient, dismissive, unreceptive tone they frequently project. **Drivers** see themselves as open to feedback and, when they don't receive any, assume it is because everyone agrees with their compelling point of view. In fact, not everyone has the **Driver's** comfort with stating agreements/disagreements and openly debating issues. Often, others conclude that it's simply not worth disagreeing with a **Driver**. At best it's uncomfortable, and it can be a no-win situation when a **Driver** is acting as though he/she has little to learn from others. However, silence does not necessarily indicate agreement, and a **Driver** may pay for his/her assumptions when resistance or passive-aggressive reactions surface later.

## *Drivers / Directors*

## Tips

- ❑ First and foremost, try to gauge how successfully or unsuccessfully you are connecting with your audience
- ❑ Check for understanding. Make sure you understand others, and they understand you. Paraphrase back what you heard others say.
- ❑ Listen. Don't rush to solve problems, offer solutions, or judge right or wrong.
- ❑ Do not interrupt or just pretend to listen until it is your turn to talk.
- ❑ Be open. Allow input and feedback. Draw others' opinions out (you may unknowingly be communicating that you don't need or want other people's input).
- ❑ Avoid monopolizing the floor. Balance speaking with respectful listening to others.
- ❑ Express appreciation. Let people know the positive impact of their contribution.
- ❑ Ask questions. **Energizers** will easily share their ideas and opinions and **Analyticals** will provide you with potentially important data if you ask them.
- ❑ Pay attention to feelings – your own and those of others – either expressed or unspoken.
- ❑ Ask for and accept help.
- ❑ Avoid projecting impatience or coming across as opinionated and others will be more willing to share their opinions and ideas.

## *Energizers / Team Builders*

## Connecting Style Description

**Energizers** have an abundance of ideas and a powerful urge to set them free. Their energy and intense focus on their audience gives them a highly-visible and powerful presence. A mutual connection is formed if their outward energy is complemented with equally powerful active listening, understanding, and appreciation of others.

Most **Energizers** have a healthy desire for recognition and approval. They strive to achieve it by sharing stories, ideas, jokes, advice, wisdom, etc. Only after they really understand the powerful impact that active listening has on engaging others, are they sufficiently motivated to make a change in the sending-receiving balance.

Fortunately, **Energizers** have the makings of excellent listeners once they – and don't take this the wrong way – get over themselves. They have the unusual ability to understand what is said and the feelings behind the words. They can skillfully summarize and reflect what they hear as well.

When frustrated, **Energizers** can come across as angry and aggressive, sometimes without realizing how personally hurtful this can feel, especially to **Supportives** and **Analyticals**.

## *Energizers / Team Builders*

# Tips

❑ Listen, listen, listen. Discipline yourself to filter what you say and how much you talk, based on your audience's style and receptivity as expressed through their body language.

❑ Speak more succinctly: state your premise and then elaborate with essential details.

❑ Pause more frequently: count to three after the other person finishes before jumping in.

❑ Draw others out: invite them to speak.

❑ Practice active listening (reflect what you heard).

❑ Make statements in a more provisional way. If you sound too certain, it discourages others from giving their opinions.

❑ Work on becoming more organized and prepared.

❑ Make sure your audience understands you. Do they need more detail, examples, and specifics?

❑ Stay on topic and stick to the schedule.

❑ Calibrate how formal or informal, touchy-feely or task-focused your approach should be based on the needs of your audience.

❑ Be very careful not to attack or criticize others when frustrated, either directly through sarcasm or indirectly with body language. It can result in people becoming defensive and annoyed. More than any other style, **Energizers** need to make sure they don't overreact emotionally.

## *Supportives / Team Players*
# Connecting Style Description

**Supportives** are typically warm, friendly, and cooperative. They enjoy working with and helping others. Relationships are extremely important to **Supportives**, who will do what they can to build and/or strengthen them. They try to accommodate the needs of others, dislike self-promotion and prefer to avoid confrontation. However, **Supportives** risk being taken advantage of due to their easy-going nature. It is sometimes difficult to know what lies beneath the friendly and accommodating surface of the **Supportive**. So, it's up to **Supportives** to share their opinions and communicate what they need or express when they are uncomfortable with someone else's behavior.

Of the four styles, Supportives are naturally the best listeners. They are genuinely interested in others, open-minded, moderate in their criticism, and appreciative of friendly interaction. The challenge for Supportives is getting their point across, especially because people of the other three styles don't make it easy for Supportives to speak their minds. If Supportives want to be treated with respect, they must learn to jump in and even ruffle feathers occasionally.

## *Supportives / Team Players*

## Tips

- ❑ Be more direct in requesting what you need from others. Don't assume people can read your mind or that they will be responsive to your needs just because you are responsive to theirs.
- ❑ Share your opinions more frequently. Don't wait to be asked. **Energizers** and **Drivers** may not always make it easy for you to claim your share of "air time," so you may have to push a little harder than people are used to seeing from you.
- ❑ Praising others is a relatively safe and highly underutilized way to show self-confidence in your opinions, e.g.,, "I really like how this is written…you make an excellent point…I am proud of our team's performance today."
- ❑ Make sure your posture, tone of voice, and eye contact match the assertive tone of your message.
- ❑ Be aware of undoing your assertive messages by minimizing their importance e.g., "This may sound silly but…don't worry, it's no big deal" or apologizing, "I hope you're not mad at me."
- ❑ Try to avoid cleaning up other people's messes and taking on roles others want to avoid.
- ❑ Avoid the tendency to take on assignments without making sure you have the clarity, resources, and support necessary to do them well. Use your right to ask questions if you are confused.
- ❑ **Supportives** feel very uncomfortable taking credit or promoting themselves and instead rely on the hope that they will be get the recognition they deserve based on the effort they put in. It's up to you to make people aware of your value.
- ❑ Don't let resentment build up inside. Take advantage of the good will and trust that you have with others by venting to friends and being direct with those whose behavior is causing the resentment.
- ❑ Allow other people to help you once in a while.

# UNIT 9.
## CONNECTING ACROSS STYLES

"Everything that irritates us about others can lead us to an understanding of ourselves."

Carl Jung

It's natural for people to be biased toward their own style, so building relationships with people of different Connecting Styles can be very frustrating. During workshops, when different style teams give each other feedback, it's rare to hear much genuine appreciation for each other's differences. Instead, there is an underlying tone of superiority suggesting that if the other style groups "were more like us," everything would work better. People seem genuinely baffled as to why the other styles would be partial to their own way of doing things.

It is unusual to see someone move out of the comfort zone of their own style to connect across styles. Most people keep behaving the same way, while harboring frustration about the other styles' annoying habits. What they don't see is how one style's behavior causes the other style to harden their defining habits. Some illustrations:

**Driver/Director**: "Why can't you **Analyticals** make a decision?"

(**Analytical**: Because you tend to make quick decisions without all the facts, which sometimes turn out to be poor decisions. It's up to us to counterbalance your impulsive behavior.)

**Analytical/Critical Thinker**: "Why can't you **Drivers** slow down long enough to hear all the facts before barreling into a final decision?"

(**Driver**: Because of your tendency toward 'analysis paralysis'. It's up to us to rescue you from yourselves.)

**Energizer/Team Builder**:  "Why don't you **Supportives** and **Analyticals** let us know where you stand?"

(**Supportives and Analyticals**:  Because you never stop talking about ideas long enough for us to get a word in edgewise.  Besides, your ideas change so frequently, why bother to take them seriously?  Why risk hurting your feelings and getting you mad at us?)

**Supportive/Team Player**:  "Why can't you **Energizers** stick to the agenda?"  (**Energizer**:  Because you **Supportives** seem to be so supportive of what we are saying, that I didn't realize at the time that you wanted me to go back to the agenda.  I thought we were having a great brainstorming session!)

No matter how well intentioned the criticisms, disapproving of and demeaning other people's styles only makes them feel more justified in their approach.  Fortunately, there is a simpler way to encourage someone with a different style to modify rather than harden their behavior and that is to mirror their style.

# Mirror Their Style and They Will Change

| If you work with... | Then... | And they will... |
|---|---|---|
| Analyticals | -Be prepared, organized and methodical<br>-Stick to business and to the facts | Relax and be more decisive |
| Drivers | -Be direct and clear<br>-Stay focused on getting results and supporting the goal | Be more inclusive |
| Supportives | -Be considerate of people's feelings<br>-Express personal interest and warmth | Share their opinions |
| Energizers | -Ask for their input and listen to their ideas<br>-Allow for socializing and express appreciation | Move more quickly toward implementation |

In the next section you will find much more detailed advice about how to connect with people based on their style.

# Unit 10.
# Guidelines for Connecting
# With Each Style

| Analyticals / Critical Thinkers |
|---|
| **Common Characteristics** |

- Task focused
- Less assertive
- Quietly determined, focused
- Loyal
- Seek autonomy and control
- Excellence driven, perfectionists
- Intellectually oriented
- Patient with complex challenges
- Good problem solvers
- Analytical
- The quietest type
- Emotionally controlled
- Serious
- Sticklers on fairness
- Private – rarely let their guard down
- Methodical and precise
- Talk slowly and quietly
- Cautious risk takers
- Cautious decision-makers
- Appreciate clarity, consistency, planning
- Sparing with appreciation and compliments
- Finish what they start (eventually)
- Critical

**Engage Analyticals By...**

- Preparing your case in advance
- Respecting their privacy, space and time
- Going through a methodical decision-making process: listing the pros/cons
- Contributing in a specific role with clear expectations for how you plan to add value
- Drawing up a step-by-step approach with no surprises
- Relying on an organized, fact-based presentation of your argument
- Planning sufficient time to do an excellent job with professional courtesies

**Avoid...**

- Being disorganized or undisciplined
- Spending time on personal issues, being too talkative or emotional
- Moving too quickly to solutions
- Being unclear about your value, role and contribution
- Leaving things to chance
- "Whining"
- Selling by manipulation or emotional appeal
- Taking shortcuts
- Pushing too hard with unrealistic deadlines

| Drivers / Directors | |
| --- | --- |
| **Common Characteristics** | |
| • Task focused<br>• More assertive<br>• Always driving toward results<br>• Quickly take charge and initiative<br>• Decisive<br>• Direct and to-the-point<br>• Strong points of view<br>• Hard working<br>• Thick skinned | • Efficient<br>• Confident<br>• Strong managers and people coordinators<br>• Willing to challenge others' ideas<br>• Responsible and dependable<br>• Independent<br>• Action oriented<br>• Low tolerance for advice and direction |

| **Engage Drivers By…** | **Avoid…** |
| --- | --- |
| • Showing mental toughness, discipline and focus on winning<br>• Showing you can outwork anyone<br>• Demonstrating self-reliance, resourcefulness and a can-do attitude<br>• Approaching them in a straightforward, direct way – sticking to business in a pleasant but professional manner<br>• Arriving at meetings prepared with a structured results-focused agenda<br>• Presenting in a clear, fact-based fashion relevant to the driver's goals and concerns<br>• Giving them bad news directly<br>• Providing them alternatives that allow them to make their own final decisions<br>• Challenging or supporting ideas, not the person<br>• Persuading with evidence<br>• Starting and ending meetings on time with professional courtesies | • Making excuses, complaining, whining, feeling sorry for yourself<br>• Rambling on or wasting time<br>• Emotional overreactions<br>• Being disorganized, improvising, or unprepared<br>• Presenting vague or unrealistic ideas not directly connected to the goal<br>• Coming across as too "touchy- feely"<br>• Expressing or taking criticism personally<br>• Persuading by personal charm or emotional appeals<br>• Going off on personal tangents or engaging them in after-hours socializing |

| Energizers / Team Builders | |
|---|---|
| **Common Characteristics** | |
| - People focused<br>- More assertive<br>- Like to express and sell their ideas to others<br>- Have an overabundance of ideas<br>- Most visionary style<br>- Bold<br>- Inspiring<br>- Best networkers<br>- Think out loud<br>- Love fun, humor and spontaneity<br>- Like to lift others' morale | - Openly express feelings and opinions<br>- Impulsive, can bite off more than they can chew<br>- Competitive high energy – will almost wear you out<br>- Want approval and recognition<br>- Risk takers<br>- Can be direct in feedback, occasionally abrasive<br>- Jump from one activity to another<br>- High energy |
| **Engage Energizers By...** | **Avoid...** |
| - Allowing them to talk about their vision and ideas without judging them<br>- Allowing for relating and socializing<br>- Being a good active listener<br>- Asking for their input and ideas<br>- Expressing appreciation<br>- Letting them know what you are feeling and thinking | - Marginalizing or ignoring their contribution; they like to be helpful<br>- Reeling in the conversation to focus on pragmatics too soon<br>- Being too impersonal<br>- Being critical<br>- Being strictly 'by the book' |

| Supportives / Team Players | |
|---|---|
| **Common Characteristics** | |
| • People focused<br>• Less assertive<br>• Team oriented<br>• Show appreciation<br>• Quiet friendliness<br>• Accommodating, helpful, supportive<br>• Good listeners<br>• Relationship builders<br>• Open and sharing<br>• Withhold critical feedback | • Modest<br>• Can appear calm even when a storm rages within<br>• Appreciate clarity and direction<br>• Industrious<br>• Implementers<br>• Service oriented<br>• Like structured, stable settings<br>• Reluctant to use authority<br>• Cautious decision makers |
| **Engage Supportives By...** | **Avoid...** |
| • Expressing personal interest, warmth and attention to relationships<br>• Expressing appreciation<br>• Being a good listener<br>• Including the people-related issues when you present your case<br>• Being organized and structured in your approach and respectful of their time<br>• Paying attention to their becoming quiet or overly accommodating – this may be a sign of concealed anger and they may need to be drawn out<br>• Avoiding direct confrontation and direct expressions of anger<br>• Approaching decisions in a participative fashion | • Sticking coldly to business<br>• Taking them for granted<br>• Forcing the conversation toward quick decisions related to your objectives<br>• Being too focused on numbers and facts and not attending to the impact of plans on people<br>• Being disorganized, inconsistent or confusing in how you approach your working relationship<br>• Bullying or being excessively abrasive or sarcastic<br>• Becoming angry and critical<br>• Being over controlling or autocratic |

# UNIT 11.
# INCREASING ROLE VERSATILITY

In the table below, place a plus sign (+) next to the role that is most natural for you and a minus sign (-) next to the role that is least natural for you. Identifying the role you are least comfortable playing will hopefully spur you on toward mastering that role. You should work to surround yourself with people who are comfortable playing the roles that you are least comfortable playing.

| Connecting Style | Team Role | Plus or Minus |
|---|---|---|
| Analytical | Critical Thinker | |
| Driver | Director | |
| Energizer | Team Leader | |
| Supportive | Team Player | |

Most of us too easily dismiss the possibility that we can be effective in roles outside of our styles. We say to ourselves: "Me, a **Driver**, become a team player in a team situation? Why that's impossible!" Or is it? The following questions are intended to help you explore the barriers to playing that new unfamiliar role, rethink some of the beliefs you've been harboring about your limitations, and challenge you to work on new behaviors that will help you become more effective in your least preferred role.

1. Imagine a situation – at work, in school, at home, or anywhere else you may be part of a team – in which it would be very important for you to play your least preferred role.

2. What aspects of that role would be hardest for you? Be as specific as you can.

**Example A:** "I am definitely a take charge woman. I am captain of the swim team, editor of the school newspaper, and active in leadership roles in many other organizations. I am on a committee with other club presidents and we often have brainstorming meetings in which I need to play the role of **Supportive–Team Player**. I am not always a good listener and can get very impatient with people who don't "get it" right away. I am quick to challenge rather than accept ideas at first. I am a <u>very direct person</u> and <u>feel like a phony when I make supportive comments to people when I don't feel they deserve it.</u> <u>I can be very critical and it shows.</u> Also, when brainstorming it is important to <u>ask questions</u> and <u>I am more comfortable giving my opinion."</u>

**Example B:** "Normally, I prefer working by myself or with a few friends who share my interests in technology, chess, and racecars. I am a volunteer EMT and there are definitely times I have to play the role of **Driver–Director**. I don't feel comfortable <u>giving orders, even though it is necessary when I am in emergency situations.</u> I <u>also like to think things through</u> and would be nervous about <u>making quick decisions</u> on behalf of my team. I am <u>concerned that people will not like me</u> or <u>blame me</u> for making decisions that some disagree with."

3. Now go back to the list of uncomfortable behaviors you've just created for question #2 and underline all the behaviors and habits that you will either have to start doing, stop doing, or do more of or less of to enable you to effectively play that role. Enter the behaviors you underlined in the left-hand column in the *Expanding My Role* worksheet on the next page, following the illustration of Example B on the following page.

## Expanding My Role

| Role I am committed to developing: DIRECTOR | | |
| --- | --- | --- |
| *Do less of or stop doing* | *Commitment* | *Proven qualities I can apply to this habit change* |
| Concerned that people will not like me or blame me | I will not let my concern that people will like me less or blame me keep me from giving my opinions and making decisions | Courage, discipline, patience |
| *Do more of or start doing* | *Commitment* | *Proven qualities I can apply* |
| Giving people orders | In emergencies, I will direct people I am responsible for even if it feels uncomfortable | Articulate, precise, even tempered |
| Making quick decisions | I will make decisions even if I do not have all the information I would normally want | Courage, knowledgeable, analytical, methodical |

## Expanding My Role

| Role I am committed to developing: | | |
| --- | --- | --- |
| *Do less of or stop doing* | *Commitment* | *Proven qualities I can apply* |
|  |  |  |
|  |  |  |
|  |  |  |
| *Do more of or start doing* | *Commitment* | *Proven qualities I can apply* |
|  |  |  |
|  |  |  |
|  |  |  |

# UNIT 12.
# ASSESSING CONNECTING STYLE IN OTHERS

Communicating across styles requires being able to accurately assess the connecting style of others, often rather quickly such as during a job interview. Recognizing Connecting Style is easiest when you assess their *assertiveness* and *task/relationship* orientation separately, rather than jumping ahead to guess their overall style. The following tables describe the observable behaviors that differentiate these two dimensions.

## Quietly or Forcefully Assertive?

| Observable Behavior | Quietly Assertive | Forcefully Assertive |
|---|---|---|
| Amount of talking | Less | More |
| Rate of talking | Slower | Faster |
| Talking volume | Softer | Louder |
| Body movement | Less, slower | More, faster |
| Posture | Relaxed/ Leans back | Leans forward |

## Task or Relationship Oriented?

| Observable Behavior | Task Oriented | Relationship Oriented |
|---|---|---|
| Uses facial animation | Less | More |
| Uses voice variation | Less | More |
| Uses animated gestures | Less | More |

#  Connecting Style Assessment Exercise

You can practice assessing *Connecting Style* in others by trying to determine which of the four styles best fits some famous people.

### Directions:

Using the two charts on the preceding page, along with the style chart on page 31, complete the matrix below to determine each person's Connecting Style by identifying:

1.  whether the person is more forcefully or quietly assertive

2.  whether the person is more relationship or task oriented

    An example has been provided for number 1.

| | Celebrity | Forcefully or Quietly Assertive | Relationship or Task Oriented | Connecting Style |
|---|---|---|---|---|
| 1 | Oprah Winfrey | Forcefully | Relationship | Energizer |
| 2 | Barak Obama | | | |
| 3 | Adam Sandler | | | |
| 4 | Bill Clinton | | | |
| 5 | Jack Nicholson | | | |

Answers on next page.

## ANSWERS:

|   | Celebrity | Assertiveness | Relationship or Task oriented | Connecting Style |
|---|-----------|---------------|-------------------------------|------------------|
| 1 | Oprah Winfrey | Forcefully | Relationship | Energizer |
| 2 | Barak Obama | Quietly | Task | Analytical |
| 3 | Adam Sandler | Quietly | Relationship | Supportive |
| 4 | Bill Clinton | Forcefully | Relationship | Energizer |
| 5 | Jack Nicholson | Forcefully | Task | Driver |

# UNIT 13.
## STYLES AT WORK

Below are examples that illustrate how the *Six Basic Connecting Needs* and *Connecting Style* can be applied to significantly enhance your personal effectiveness. Note that in each of these interactions, disconnects related to style differences between well-intentioned people can quickly become highly emotional, personal, and destructive conflicts that undermine relationships and impact business results.

## 1. A Supportive and Analytical in Conflict

When Nat first joined the department, Mark, his supervisor, was very friendly and supportive. Their group was in a small open area where four people worked in close proximity. When Nat's father got sick, Mark went out of his way to support him by accommodating his schedule, driving him places when necessary, and generally making himself available. Yet, as much as he appreciated Mark's support, Nat began to feel uncomfortable. His need for privacy and space grew, and his stress level mounted. He began spending more time away from his desk and when he was in the common work area, he was less socially responsive. Mark took this personally. He felt unappreciated and hurt and made the mistake of raising the issue as a work-related concern by insisting that Nat act more friendly (for the benefit of office morale) and that he let Mark know where he was at all times "in case customers called asking for him," all of which seemed bogus and highly offensive to Nat's need for privacy. Nat, in turn, became even more remote and outright irritated with Mark. Once things had escalated, their personal dynamics seemed to reverse: Mark went from going out of his way to make life as comfortable for Nat as possible, to making him quite uncomfortable.

Mark, a **Supportive**, started out by treating Nat the way he would like to have been treated if he were in the same situation – with warmth, support, and increased availability. Nat, an **Analytical**, valued privacy and control and simply needed some space. The harder Mark tried, the more Nat needed to pull away. As Nat picked up resentment from Mark, he felt threatened and even more remote.

What went wrong?

1.  Lack of understanding each other's *Connecting Style* and how to connect based on style

2.  Assuming bad intentions when the other felt treated in a way that made them uncomfortable

3.  Being unresponsive to the following key needs that lead to a strong connection:

4.  Nat's need to feel understood, respected, autonomous (allowing him to feel in control), included, and trusted.

5.  Mark's need to feel valued, included, and understood.

How could this have been avoided?

- If Mark asked Nat how he could be most helpful at this difficult time, it would have supported Nat's needs.

- If Nat expressed appreciation for Mark's extending himself, it would have met Mark's needs and would have helped him relax.

# 2. Drivers – The hard road from loner to leader

Making the transition from an individual technical contributor to manager can be difficult. A new manager must redefine personal and professional effectiveness to include not only technical excellence, but also the ability to motivate, assess, develop, and influence people individually and collectively.

Some of the most technically gifted and individually effective managers have had their careers sidelined indefinitely by their inability to develop people skills.

People with such qualities as competitiveness, independence, aggression, dominance, and the need for control – some of the very traits traditionally associated with individual corporate success – seem especially vulnerable.

Roger, a **Driver** with **Analytical** secondary style, was an engineer in a consumer products company. He was assigned to be a project manager less than a year out of school. He had a reputation for hard work, unmatched business knowledge, unflinching competitiveness, and a quick, intuitive, steel trap mind.

Roger usually worked independently or with a small team of like style peers. His accomplishments had earned him a reputation as someone who could get things done. With his highly competitive and aggressive style, he soon became a favorite of the boss, clearing the way for a fast trek up the ladder to manager within a few short years out of school.

But Roger was developing a reputation for being impossible to work with. As far as he was concerned, there was his way and the wrong way. He was a black-and-white thinker who hid his vulnerabilities behind a mask of total self-reliance, confidence, and control. He was available to those who needed his help, but he showed little patience for opinions, approaches, or work styles that differed from his own.

Ironically, Roger's colleagues saw the competitive, aggressive style for which Roger had been so well rewarded as insensitivity, defensiveness, and over control. His intimidating style compelled others to feign agreement with him or avoid him. That pattern, along with his tendency to surround himself with like-style individuals as his closest subordinates, enabled Roger to maintain an unrealistically positive view of himself as a project manager. In the meantime, he had created a highly repressive atmosphere in which most team members felt devalued and underutilized.

In time, disaffection and turnover increased among his staff as did complaints to the human resource manager. Morale was low, and with it loyalty, creativity, and innovation.

Encouraged by his human resource manager, Roger began to practice a more participatory style of management. For example, he tried delegating more responsibility to subordinates, but he was too anxious about giving up control to allow his people to take approaches different than the ones he preferred. Rather than truly allowing autonomy, he continued to rescue, control, and second guess people on his team – in effect, undermining their confidence and authority. This pressure brought out the worst in his people and reinforced his excuse for not being more participative: "They are not ready for it."

**A successful transformation**: Over the next four years, Roger was passed up several times for promotions and transferred laterally to other areas. Then the roof caved in. A peer steadfastly refused to work with him, and his mentor retired.

Now Roger was read the riot act: "We value you, need you and want you, but your career now depends on your ability to work effectively with others. People-handling skills are now the bottom line."

With the help of an executive coach, Roger made good progress in the developmental objectives judged critical to his success (improved skills in listening, conflict resolution, assertion, and consensus building). He became more sharply aware of his blind spots and the effect of his behavior on others. His personality did not change dramatically, but he was able to modify enough of the dysfunctional behaviors to make a difference in his effectiveness.

# 3. Energizers: Listen to your audience

**Energizers** are known as visionaries with a natural ability to inspire, motivate and engage others. Just as **Energizers'** strengths can be larger than life, so can their blind spots. As I learned during one of my earliest consulting assignments, when **Energizers** become too passionate about their ideas, they risk losing touch with their audience and engagement turns into disaffection.

Rose (**Energizer**) was a charismatic sales manager who asked me to help her understand why her sales force (largely service oriented **Supportives**) was failing to sell a new, highly profitable investment product to their customers. From her perspective, this was a product they requested, and one she went out on a limb to get funded.

As is typical of **Energizers**, her response to the poor results was blaming and attacking. "They are the ones who asked for this. They couldn't wait to get it. Are these the right sales people? Maybe we should replace a few with stronger people."

Extensive interviewing revealed a major disconnect. Her sales people did not believe in this product from the start. Trained to be

67

customer focused, they had lots of doubts about how beneficial it would be, despite its profitability to their firm. It is true that Rose heard a lot of enthusiasm, but the apparent buy-in was mostly a function of people's perception that she was in love with the strategy, had already made up her mind, and disagreeing would be hazardous to their continued employment. And yet Rose was incredulous to learn that her employees had not openly shared their differences with her. "I told my people a thousand times that my door is always open and I want honest feedback."

Taking her up on her wish to be perfectly honest, I suggested that while she thought her sales force was totally on-board with this product, their desire to please her kept them from sharing their deep concerns and objections. I also shared with her my doubts that replacing staff would solve the problem.

**Lessons learned:** The more powerful an **Energizer's** passion, the harder they have to work at getting people to share their independent opinions. Recall that the keys to influence include supporting others' needs to feel understood, included, appreciated, respected and autonomous. In this case, none of these needs were supported and the connection between Rose and her sales team never happened. This would have been the case across all styles, but it is especially true of **Supportives**. Apart from being self-protective, **Supportives** are reluctant to burst other people's bubbles. If they have doubts about what they hear from an **Energizer**, they are just as likely to dismiss their doubts as trust them. Rose needed to work hard to get genuine buy-in. She would have had a much easier time of it had she allowed the sales force to be involved in creating the new product. **Supportives** need to take more risks in giving voice to their opinions and doubts. Their naturally non-threatening style and sensitivity to others' pride makes their voice the easiest for **Energizers** to hear. Still, you **Supportives** should expect a defensive reaction at first and not let it discourage you from asserting your opinion.

As if to confirm the accuracy of my findings and the instincts of her sales force, she thanked me for my excellent assessment and promptly replaced me with a consultant who was smart enough to agree with her. By the way, the fact that I am also an **Energizer** may have contributed to her difficulty digesting my findings. If I had to do it again, I would have spent a lot more time asking her questions and allowing her to give voice to her frustrations prior to sharing a report.

# PART THREE

# Twenty-First Century Self-Empowerment Skills

As the following poem makes clear, the first stop on the road to success is having a firm grip on reality.

*There's a Hole in My Sidewalk*
By Portia Nelson[2]

I

I walk down the street.
There is a deep hole in the sidewalk.
I fall in.
I am lost…I am helpless.
It isn't my fault.
It takes forever to find a way out.

II

I walk down the same street.
There is a deep hole in the sidewalk.
I pretend I don't see it.
I fall in again.
I can't believe I am in the same place.
But, it isn't my fault.
It still takes a long time to get out.

III

I walk down the same street.
There is a deep hole in the sidewalk.
I see it is there.
I still fall in.  It's a habit.
My eyes are open.
I know where I am.
It is my fault.  I get out immediately.

IV

I walk down the same street.
There is a deep hole in the sidewalk.
I walk around it.

V

I walk down another street.

# UNIT 14.
## LISTENING

"Yeah, I called her up; she gave me a bunch of crap
about me not listening to her or something. I don't know, I
wasn't really paying attention."

(Harry in the movie, Dumb and Dumber, 1994, New Line Cinema)

Listening is the single most important skill to a successful and satisfying work life. Yet more people, including most of those in the highest leadership positions, rank listening as their greatest weakness.

Nothing you can do, short of saving someone's life, creates a more powerful bond than giving someone the feeling that you understand him or her without judgment. Whether it is your boss, peer, customer, or friend, when another person says about you, "she really gets me," you are on your way to go-to guy/girl status. When it comes to supporting the six basic needs, listening, directly or indirectly, supports every one, whereas expressing great ideas supports virtually none of those needs, unless it is a response to a specific request.

The need to feel listened to and understood is as powerful as the need for food and water. The skillful listening of a psychotherapist can help heal emotional damage, whereas ignoring or invalidating can actually cause emotional damage. In fact, many societies consider ignoring a person, in the form of *shunning,* a punishment worse than death. In the workplace, few things are more upsetting than being ignored or unnoticed.

Expect to run into very few good listeners over the course of your career. The only good news is that it gives you a great opportunity to distinguish yourself by honing your listening skills. In a sample of over one thousand middle to senior managers, the single most common development need was to become a better listener. It is as if we have trouble with the idea that other people will value being listened to as much as we do.

Most leaders and managers are poor listeners. How many people in your life modeled good listening?

When did anyone ever win a political debate because they were the better listener?

Know anyone on the high school listening team?

The kind of listening that leads to successful relationship building is very different from what most of us do most of the time. Let's look at the different levels of listening to develop awareness of how we listen and the impact effective listening has upon success.

## Levels of Listening

We all operate at different levels of listening at different times. At the higher levels, our minds are more focused, and we have greater perspective and access to our wisdom. Being able to listen effectively is key to learning about the organization, learning what is expected, ensuring you are doing the right thing, and building collaborative relationships.

Research suggests that one of the contributing factors to higher levels of listening is that our minds are free of distractions. Let's take a look at how this works. The table below shows different and distinct levels of listening. In real life the levels overlap and interact in different ways. As you go through this table, think about what levels are familiar to you, ones that you recognize and use frequently.

| Level | Description and Interpersonal Impact |
|---|---|
| **LOWEST LEVEL** Non-listening | Have you ever had so much on your mind that you completely missed what someone was saying? A busy, preoccupied mind is like a computer in which the hard drive is totally full. No more information can be processed. |
| Listening to tell my story | At this level, you are operating from memory instead of in the moment. Someone may say something that triggers a memory. You listen just enough to hear the topics you want to talk about. You hear the word *vacation* and you launch into a narrative about your week at the shore. |
| Listening to argue or disagree | In this level, you are caught up in disagreement or agreement. When this occurs, you are steeped in memory. You're judging and comparing based on your beliefs from the past and are not truly listening.<br><br>Here is how that happens. Let's say you are talking with a colleague, Mary, about an idea for a needed improvement. As Mary describes her idea, she says something that you disagree with and you start to formulate a rebuttal. Instead of really listening, you think about what you're going to say next. You may even have a negative emotional reaction toward Mary. All this time, Mary is still talking and saying things that might have some merit. While your mind is occupied with thoughts of what to say next and you're experiencing negative feelings, what happens to your ability to listen? *It is reduced.*<br><br>The same thing happens if you agree with what's being said. Your mind jumps ahead to what to say next. The more you're gripped by being in a state of agreement/disagreement with the person you're listening to and the more you're thinking about a response, the less effectively you listen to what's being said in the moment. In fact, you miss much of what is being said and people will experience the suffocating effect of negativity upon new ideas, creativity and innovation. |

| Level | Description and Interpersonal Impact |
|---|---|
| **MID-LEVEL** Listening for application | As your mind quiets down for the business of noting all the things you agree and disagree with, you get to a higher level of listening. At this level, you are examining the information for application. You might be asking yourself, "What does this information mean to me?" or "How might I make use of what I am hearing?" This type of thinking can be characterized as logical and linear. You will tend to make comparisons between what you are hearing and what you know from your past experiences or what you expect the future will hold. In this state, your mind will be quite active. You are usually pretty sure that you accurately understand what you are hearing. You might even be quite righteous in your opinion that you know exactly what they mean. |
| Listening for implication | Once you've applied the message and your mind quiets down a bit more, you might find yourself thinking, "What are the larger implications of what I am hearing?" The personal level has increased and the mind is even quieter. At this level, you begin to translate what you are hearing as it applies to your life rather than to only work. The insight is deeper and you see how the things that are being said have meaning for you and your life. There is a willingness to be curious about what you are hearing and an increasing openness or sensitivity toward the person to whom you are listening. Preconceived notions do not exist. You are starting to see with greater perspective. You are beginning to consider options that you had not noticed before. |

| Level | Description and Interpersonal Impact |
|---|---|
| **HIGHEST LEVEL** Listening to Understand | At the listening for understanding level, you are present to hear not only the entire message, but you pick up on the subtleties of communication. In this state, you are able to hear the entire message without distractions. This can be as simple as listening for the entire message in order to get directions or as complex as listening to someone's point of view on how to rid the country of violence.<br><br>When your mind quiets down, you find that an even deeper level of listening becomes available to you. At this level, you not only hear and understand the entire message of what you are being told, you also begin to gain some insight into and an understanding of the state of mind of the person to whom you are listening. You get a sense of the meaning that exists beyond the words. As this occurs, you can see people and events in your life with greater perspective and you may have incredible insights about the most effective action to take. |

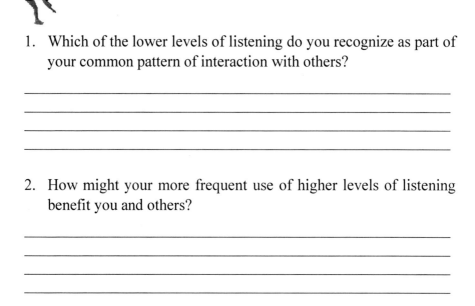

1. Which of the lower levels of listening do you recognize as part of your common pattern of interaction with others?

   _____

   _____

   _____

   _____


2. How might your more frequent use of higher levels of listening benefit you and others?

   _____

   _____

   _____

   _____

# Listening Conveys Confidence

Listening, like empathy, has become associated with weakness and lack of decisiveness.

That's what US Navy Captain Michael Abrashoff thought until he worked for Admiral William Perry. In *It's Your Ship: Management Techniques from the Best Damn Ship in the Navy, (New York, NY: Warner Books, 2002,)* Abrashoff writes about Perry:

*"He was universally loved and admired by heads of state, by ministers of defense and foreign affairs, and by our own and our ally's troops. A lot of that was because of the way he listened. Each person who talked to him had his complete, undivided attention. Everyone blossomed in his presence, because he was so respectful, and I realized I wanted to affect people the same way...*

*It was painful, but crucial for my realization, that listening doesn't always come naturally to me. Perry opened my eyes to how often I just pretended to hear people. I wasn't paying attention; I was marking time until it was my turn to give orders."*

Ben Franklin recognized that listening to the other person's ideas plus resisting the urge to share your own pearls of wisdom creates the highest level of receptivity:

"Would you win the hearts of others, you must not seem to vie with them but to admire them. Give them every opportunity of displaying their own qualifications and when you have indulged their vanity they will praise you in turn and prefer you above others. Such is the vanity of mankind that minding what others say is a much surer way of pleasing them than talking well ourselves."

For an Energizer like Franklin, listening was an active struggle. "When another asserted something I thought in error, I denied myself the pleasure of contradicting him." And while usually the smartest person in the room, he realized that "...even the smartest comments would occasion envy and disgust..."

So far, we've talked about listening as the foundation to relationship building and communication effectiveness. The other reason listening is critical may be so obvious as to overlook it. You learn important things when you listen.

Good listening starts with an accurate self-assessment of your listening habits and identification of the skills you wish to develop. For this purpose we have provided a Listening Habit Self-Assessment on the next page. Take a moment to read the directions and complete this very brief survey.

## Listening Habit Self-Assessment

**Directions for Scoring**: Rate yourself on how often you demonstrate each of the following listening habits by placing an X in the appropriate box (Often, Sometimes, Rarely). Count the number of X's in each column and enter the total number in line 19. Multiply the number in line 19 by the number in line 20. Enter the result in line 21. Add the three scores together from line 21 and enter the total in line 22. Refer to the key following the survey to determine your level of effectiveness as a listener.

| Listening Habits | 1 Often | 2 Some-times | 3 Rarely |
|---|---|---|---|
| 1. Listening when I have a clear mind and few distractions. | | | |
| 2. Listening with attentive posture, good eye contact and lots of encouraging non-verbal feedback. | | | |
| 3. Listening quietly. | | | |
| 4. Letting a few seconds go by after another person stops talking before speaking. (People are very eager to fill silence.) | | | |
| 5. Using door openers to encourage opening up – nodding or saying, "go on…I see…say more". | | | |
| 6. Paraphrasing what I hear in terms of both the content and the emotions of the message. | | | |
| 7. Asking questions that focus on helping them talk it through – rather than solving the problem for them. | | | |
| 8. Genuine, as opposed to fake, listening. | | | |
| 9. Listening while ignoring other things, i.e.,, not answering the phone, not looking at my watch. | | | |
| 10. Not interrupting to say something I may think is more important. | | | |
| 11. Not finishing their sentences even if I think I know what they want to say. | | | |
| 12. Not interrupting to disagree. | | | |
| 13. Not judging the importance of what they are saying. | | | |
| 14. Listening without formulating my rebuttal. | | | |
| 15. Listening until they are done speaking regardless of whether I have come up with a solution or advice beforehand. | | | |
| 16. Not interrupting to share my story. "I have it worse…" | | | |
| 17. Not asking irrelevant questions. | | | |
| 18. Not judging –not thinking or saying, "Why did you do that?, You brought it on yourself!" etc. | | | |
| 19. SUBTOTAL | | | |
| 20. MULTIPLIER | x1 | x2 | x3 |
| 21. SCORE FOR COLUMN | | | |
| 22. TOTAL SCORE | | | |

## KEY:

| Score | Effective Listener |
|-------|--------------------|
| 18-24 | Effective Listener |
| 25-34 | Somewhat effective, room for improvement |
| 35-42 | Borderline ineffective, time for a tune up |
| 43-54 | Ineffective, time for an overhaul so Listen Up! |

# Unit 15.
# Self-Directed Learning

"Learn of the skillful; he that teaches himself, has a fool for his master."

Benjamin Franklin

One of the most critical early career success factors is your ability to learn on your own. Your performance will be judged based on how fast, how much, and how deeply you can gain an understanding of your job, department, company, culture, people, industry and yourself. The ability to continuously learn, adapt and change differentiates top performers in every phase of one's career. But you will never be on a steeper learning curve than when you enter the workplace for the first time.

Let's face it – after being a student for all but two or three years of your life so far, you are probably more than ready to apply what you have learned. Many begin their careers so eager to unleash the solutions and skills they learned in school, internships and prior work experiences that they miss critical opportunities to learn and understand everything they can by unleashing their curiosity through listening, researching, reading, observing, and asking questions.

Just as *good* is the enemy of *great*, *knowledge* can be the enemy of *learning*, especially for achievement motivated individuals who are transitioning from a highly competitive school system into the highly competitive workplace. By all appearances, being an expert and having the answers appears much more important to rapid career growth than acknowledging ignorance and asking questions.

*"You should enter every project humbly and a little dumb. So long as you don't stay dumb. There's nothing wrong with that. And you'll obviously need to have your ego checked. Find out what you don't know. Like we said earlier, humility clears the path, but curiosity, curiosity is the driving force..."* Dave Marcum, Steve Smith and Mahan Khalsa, *BusinessThink, Rules for Getting It Right – Now and No Matter What*. John Wiley and Sons, Inc. New York, 2002.

In fact, the most common sources of failure for CEO's and entry level employees alike are arrogance, the addiction to being right, and distaste for uncertainty – all part and parcel of being a highly competitive person. There is a certain feeling of control, invulnerability, strength and pride that accompanies mastery. The problem is that having more expertise than anyone in the room is not the same as mastery. Take it from Albert Einstein – *"The difference between what the most and the least learned people know is inexpressibly trivial in relation to that which is unknown."* Even when you do finally achieve mastery, in today's globalized, information rich world, no sooner do you achieve subject-matter mastery than your subject matter becomes obsolete. The ability and willingness to learn continuously is the differentiator.

> "A *good* listener is not only popular everywhere, but after a while he knows something."
>
> Wilson Mizner, 1876-1933

In addition to giving you the information you will need to succeed, entering your new workplace as a "student" will make you more popular by satisfying all *Six Basic Connecting Needs* (described on pages 16-18). By seeking information, guidance and insights in a genuine way, you give people the chance to feel helpful, valued, respected, understood and included. This initial experience of you will lead others to want to spend time with you and be more open to your contributions. However, if you try to contribute without having built this foundation, you risk coming across as dangerously competitive and self-interested, and people will close down and/or shut you out.

Yet being the kind of open-minded learner that fits the global workplace is not easy, given how human nature programs us, our school systems condition us, and the workplace rewards us.

Many of us leave the highly competitive academic culture addicted to *knowing* and uncomfortable accessing and owning up to our ignorance (the precursor to all learning). Acknowledging just how much you do not know can be extremely unnerving, especially if, like Drivers and Energizers, you are the type who hates to ask for directions when you are lost.

Strange though it may be, school teaches us to value certainty over curiosity:

| Rewarded and Encouraged | Not Rewarded and Discouraged |
|---|---|
| ☐ Having the right or best answer<br>☐ Being confident or certain about your answer<br>☐ Being able to defend your answer<br>☐ Coming up with a solution that is better than anyone else's | ☐ Admitting that you need to know more before arriving at a solution<br>☐ Admitting to being uncertain<br>☐ Feeling that your solution can be improved<br>☐ Being interested in what other people come up with and using that to make your solution better<br>☐ Being prepared with the questions that will lead to a better answer |

Most corporate cultures send mixed signals about the value of learning. While billions of dollars are invested in employee learning and training, the vast majority of time is spent getting stuff done – not reviewing lessons learned, incorporating best practices from outside of the company, and learning how to do things better. Very few leaders, managers, and teams have the inner confidence and humility to acknowledge how much they do not know, to honestly come to terms with their performance gaps, and create a culture of continuous improvement.

Success research tells us that in the real world, the higher up the ladder people go, the more likely they are to become know-it-alls and surround themselves with people who think the same way and will not challenge them. The management teams they build beneath them fall in love with their way of doing things and quickly create walls that prevent people from challenging their treasured assumptions. Rather than develop a culture of continuous learning and improvement, most workplaces develop cultures that protect and deepen the status quo.

These attitudes toward learning quickly trickle down through the culture and have an impact felt even at entry levels. The more the workplace is a learning organization, the more it will be a teaching organization. Learning-oriented companies pay a lot of attention to the training and development they provide to interns and new employees. They attract and develop managers who spend time teaching, mentoring, coaching and giving feedback.

Unfortunately learning organizations are far and few between. Be prepared to take your learning and development into your own hands. The guidance provided in Section 2, *Learn and adapt quickly* (page 124), of The Eight Keys to Early Career Success will be very helpful. In addition, the Career Entry Checklist in Unit 22 provides a specific and easy-to-use approach to starting in a new company as a self-directed learner.

How would you describe your strengths and weaknesses as a self-directed learner? Write down two strengths and two weaknesses below.

Strengths:

1 _____

_____

_____

_____

2 _____

_____

_____

_____

Weaknesses:

1 _____

_____

_____

_____

2 _____

_____

_____

_____

# UNIT 16.
## SELF-DISCIPLINE

*"In reading the lives of great men, I found that the first victory they won was over themselves...self-discipline with all of them came first."* Harry S. Truman

If brainpower is the engine that drives success, self-discipline is the steering wheel, brake and accelerator. Comprised of the ability to delay immediate gratification to achieve longer-term success, overcome laziness and procrastination, and persevere over time and in the face of adversity, self-discipline is essential to directing your own path.

Imagine that you are four years old, seated next to a plate of luscious marshmallows. An adult tells you that he is leaving the room and that when he returns in several minutes, he will give you two marshmallows. Then he offers you an alternative: you can ring a bell any time and he will return immediately and give you one marshmallow, but only one. What would you do? Would you go for the one marshmallow "in the hand" or wait for two "in the bush?"

This was exactly the predicament dozens of children found themselves in as participants in the now famous study conducted in the 1960's at Stanford University by psychologist Walter Mischel. His Marshmallow Study is commonly cited as strongly supporting the idea that good things come to those who wait.

Subjects were followed up 14 years later, at age 18. As expected, the students who delayed gratification during the initial study were more successful students later in life, as measured by higher SAT scores, better self-control, planning, and an ability to persevere in the face of minor setbacks.

The Marshmallow Study is a perfect metaphor for the internal struggle we all face. As I write this sentence, I wonder – should I take a break and do some shopping on line (one marshmallow)? Or should I discipline myself to finish this section, which will make me feel much better about myself in the long run (two marshmallows)?

For those of you who imagine your four-year-old selves giving in to temptation, as adults you probably have to work extra hard to discipline yourself. You may be more prone to procrastinating, to excessive partying, overeating, and not being fully aware of the consequences of putting things off or indulging your fun zone.

For those who imagine your four-year-old selves successfully holding out for the two marshmallows, congratulations. Self-discipline is probably one of your strengths and has likely contributed to your success. But it is possible to overuse self-control and undermine your success as in those who lean toward becoming compulsive and a perfectionist – a precursor to becoming a workaholic or a control freak, and even lead to eating disorders like anorexia and bulimia. Over control can also interfere with the emotional openness essential to building strong relationships.

Going to college is like the Marshmallow Study on steroids. Not only are you constantly struggling between short-term gratification and long-term success, but in college you are surrounded by friends who seem determined to convince you to go for the one marshmallow instead of waiting for two.

Developing your self-discipline in college will serve you well in preparing for the workplace where the challenges are ratcheted up a few notches and the stakes are higher. The following are just some of the countless *marshmallow* decisions you will be faced with every day:

- Should I stay late and finish this project or work out at the gym?

- Should I review this report one more time for typos or print it out?

- Should I share gossip about one colleague to another or keep it to myself?

- Should I watch TV or prepare for tomorrow's meeting?

- Should I complain about how bored I am in this job or keep it to myself and see how I can make it more interesting?

- Should I move to a bigger apartment and live paycheck to paycheck or stay where I am and save some money?

- Should I tell my colleague off now in front of everyone, or wait and think about a constructive approach to expressing my frustration?

The very high rate of business decision failure – at least 50% – is due to smart people impulsively implementing the first solution that seems to make sense (one marshmallow) rather than waiting until they understand the problem and its causes and implementing an effective solution (two marshmallows). Constant pressure from the marketplace, media, shareholders, consumers, boards, and senior managers for short-term results puts subtle pressure on every employee to implement any solution they could rather than hold off and implement the solution they should.

While young Americans enter college and the workplace with a leg up in the communication, technical, political, and innovative arenas, many have a natural disadvantage. They lack the resolve to persevere through hardship and make sacrifices. The message from parents, politicians, and consumer-driven media is that, "You can and should have it all. Take what is yours. Buy that house or that car now. You deserve it. If you can qualify for that low-cost mortgage and credit card, you can afford it. Don't worry about consequences – someone will bail you out. Don't worry about excessive partying – you can always check into rehab. There are no permanent consequences to your decisions. The main thing is to enjoy life."

The collateral damage of our relative affluence is that, as a country, we act as though we can have one marshmallow right away <u>and</u> the other two later. The consequence for young people entering the workforce is the culture shock of finding themselves at the bottom of the pecking order where their self-discipline will be seriously tested by frustration of strenuous but tedious assignments, long thankless hours, cleaning up other people's messes, etc. In the meantime, they will be competing with highly self-disciplined young professionals from around the globe who, like many of our parents and grandparents, associate work with literal survival and grew up with a radically higher frustration threshold.

So no matter how hard you feel you are working and putting up with an unfavorable environment, discipline yourself to hold off a little longer before grabbing for the marshmallow. You can do it. marshmallow.

How would you describe your strengths and weaknesses when it comes to self-discipline?    Write down two strengths and two weaknesses below.

Strengths:

1_____

_____

_____

_____

2_____

_____

_____

_____

_____

Weaknesses:

1_____

_____

_____

_____

2_____

_____

_____

_____

# UNIT 17.
## HABIT CHANGE

The ability to translate self-awareness into behavior change is essential to a successful career. There are few experiences more satisfying or more critical to building confidence and self-esteem than developing a new skill or giving up a bad habit when we know we should. Conversely, repeated experiences of trying and failing to change behavior leads to what psychologists call 'learned helplessness' which, over time, leads to a victimized, vulnerable and resentful orientation toward one's career and life.

In the unpredictable and rapidly changing global workplace, you must be prepared to adapt or risk being left behind. Adapting is nothing more than a combination of giving up old habits and learning and mastering new ones. The 21$^{st}$ century self-empowerment skills covered earlier – listening (for feedback), self-discipline and self-directed learning – provide the foundation for self-directed behavioral change. However, even with that foundation, achieving long-term behavior change is very difficult.

How many New Year's resolutions did you stick to versus give up on? How many times did you promise yourself to never lose your temper again, stop saying "yes" when you mean "no," give up smoking, only to go right back to the old habits? Being aware that a habit is counterproductive is often not enough to get us to change. In extreme cases, realizing that if you do not change your behavior you might die – as in smoking, may not be enough to get a person to change.

On the other hand, the idea that people do not change – "we are who we are" – is patently false. All human beings develop skills and change habits over the course of their lives. Even if it takes you five failed attempts to stop smoking before you stop for good, the bottom line is that you changed a habit.

People develop new skills and behaviors either because they have to, or because they choose to. When they choose to, it isn't necessarily because they have been "wrong"; it is because they want to be more effective. For a change you *have to* make (to survive), the environment and circumstances provide the motivation necessary to get past the inconveniences, anxiety, and discomfort that long-term habit change involves. For change *you choose to make*, the motivation and determination must come from you. Self-directed behavior change is much more challenging and far more prone to failure. Knowing what to expect on the road to change and being able to anticipate those points along the way where people's efforts are most likely to derail can give you a real advantage.

# The Road to Behavior Change

We all know that habit change is never easy. The table and description below describe the temporary dip in comfort and effectiveness that occurs from the time you discover the negative impact of a longstanding habit until you reach the point when the new behavior becomes automatic.

**Road To Change**

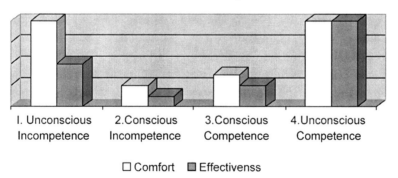

| I. Unconscious Incompetence | 2.Conscious Incompetence | 3.Conscious Competence | 4.Unconscious Competence |

□ Comfort  ■ Effectivenss

**IN THE COMFORT ZONE:**

**Phase 1. Unconscious Incompetence**: You are <u>unaware</u> of those aspects of your behavior that are counterproductive.

Frank's sarcasm was described as "part of his charm" to friends who knew him well, but to others on his team his sarcasm was experienced as insulting and demeaning. It was so engrained in his style that he was unaware that he was sarcastic at all. Frank was in the "ignorance is bliss" phase of development. What you don't know about yourself can't hurt you. In fact, he was alienating a number of colleagues until eventually, his supervisor gave him provided feedback that his sarcasm was hurting his performance and he would have to change. This feedback moved Frank out of the comfort zone and into conscious incompetence.

## OUTSIDE THE COMFORT ZONE:

**Phase 2. Conscious Incompetence**: You become <u>aware</u> of the counterproductive behaviors and feel uncomfortably self-conscious and awkward.

Frank went from carefree, natural and self-assured in how he spoke to colleagues to constantly self-doubting and worried about how he was coming across. Not exactly sure how he was coming across, his self-censoring was making him feel vulnerable and ineffective. With no outlet for communicating his disagreement, he was extremely frustrated. Had it not been for his supervisor's insistence that he work on disagreeing more respectfully, he would have quickly lapsed back to his old habits. As Frank began to understand which phrases were particularly problematic for colleagues (for example, "yeah right", "try again" "another brilliant idea") and learn techniques for disagreeing in an agreeable way, he moved to the third phase of behavioral change, which is conscious competence.

## OUTSIDE THE COMFORT ZONE:

**Phase 3. Conscious Competence**: You become conscious of the things you can do to be effective, but incorporating them makes you feel self-conscious and uncomfortable.

In this phase, Frank might read a self-help book, take a workshop, get coaching from his manager or friend and observe effective people, all the while developing a menu of tools and techniques that he could imagine using. He might spend time doing various exercises such as developing scripts for what he might say instead of being sarcastic, practice with friends, and eventually try it out in real life situations. No matter how much sense these new techniques might make, it still feels very forced, awkward and ineffective. If Frank gets this far and can practice over and over again, whatever new habits he is working on would start to become automatic. When that happens, Frank is in Phase 4, Unconscious Competence.

## IN THE COMFORT ZONE:

**Phase 4. Unconscious Competence**: The new skills finally become unconscious again or "habit" and you are effective and comfortable.

Being aware of the challenges you will face in changing your behavior is only one of the keys to successful long-term change. On the following page you will find recommendations to ensure successful long-term behavior change:

## *The Keys to Successful Behavior Change*

1.  Select one or at most two behaviors to tackle at a time. One of the biggest mistakes people make is biting off more than they can chew. Even something as simple as becoming a more effective listener is likely to require a tremendous amount of sustained focus to achieve.

2.  Be absolutely certain that you are ready to commit. Successful habit change comes long after we realize that a habit is counterproductive. There needs to be enough evidence from the feedback you get that: a) links specific behavior with the negative impact, b) your behavior is hurtful or counterproductive to others or yourself, and c) that if you don't change, you will not be able to achieve results that are very important to you or you risk losing someone or something that is very important to you. In the case of listening, reminding yourself of "the bigger prize", avoiding derailment, provides internal motivation. Much the way substance abusers don't change until they hit rock bottom, habit change does not occur until lots of negative feedback directly tied to that behavior makes us reach a tipping point. While you might become aware of many things to do more of or less of as you read the handbook, there are probably just a few habits that are ripe for the changing.

3.  Do not wait for the workplace culture to support and reinforce the habits you are aiming for. Andrea has committed to becoming more inclusive, while her boss and her boss's boss manage autocratically. James is working on being more appreciative in spite of the fact that the last two promotions were for people who almost never offer praise. Most habit change occurs with the organizational current in your face.

4.  Make sure the behavior you want to change is specific. "Being a better listener", "exercising more" or "being more positive" are all very broad concepts that are made up of a number of specific behaviors and habits. For example, "allowing other people to finish their thoughts" is one of several habit changes that will lead to being a more effective listener. (If you go to the Listening

Habits Self-Assessment on page 81 you will find several other such habits.) Focusing on each habit separately is the way to go.

5. Recognize that you have a choice in every decision you make. When you tell yourself that you no longer have to respond to people in your usual way just because that is the way you have been responding for many years, you have come a long way toward change.

6. Let others know what you are trying to achieve. Not only will making your development goals public add to your incentive to persevere, it is likely to motivate others to be more supportive.

7. Work from a realistic, structured development plan that clearly defines your goals, the steps necessary to get there, and a means of gathering feedback along the way. Development Planning forms can be found on pages 153-160.

1. Write down two lifestyle or habit changes you successfully made (quitting a bad habit like smoking, starting or sustaining a healthy habit or lifestyle change).

_____

_____

_____

_____

_____

_____

a. What was the hardest part of making that change?

_____

_____

_____

_____

_____

_____

_____

_____

b. To what do you attribute your success?

_____

_____

_____

_____

_____

_____

_____

_____

2. Think of two lifestyle or habit changes you were not able to successfully make.

_____

_____

_____

_____

_____

a. To what do you attribute your failure to make the change?

_____

_____

_____

_____

_____

_____

_____

_____

_____

# UNIT 18.
## NETWORKING

Tom Friedman's description of the highly globalized or "flat world" in which we all live underscores just how critical developing a strong network is to career success: *"Around the year 2000 we entered a whole new [globalized] era...the thing that gives it its unique character is the new found power for individuals to collaborate and compete globally...individuals must and can ask 'where do I fit into the global competition and opportunities of the day and how can I, on my own, collaborate with others globally?'"* If you are not connected through a global network of relationships, you may as well be working in a cave.

Building a strong network as early in your career as possible gives you a distinct competitive advantage because it:

- <u>maximizes your value added</u>. Unlike technical, analytical and customer service roles, which are those most likely to be outsourced, networking skills that give you access to key industry players make you indispensable.

- <u>gives you true career mobility</u>. It is the best way of finding a job. By some estimates, more than 70% of all jobs are filled through informal networking channels. Even when you have a good job, a strong network is critical to remaining abreast of global trends and opportunities you may wish or need to take advantage of at any given time. Your network allows for career mobility and freedom of choice so that the many job and company changes you are likely to make over your lifetime will be made with you in the driver's seat. The information you get from your network will help you to understand your world from an external perspective and make you more aware of critical market trends, what is going on in the job market, what skills are most in demand, and what jobs are most and least vulnerable to outsourcing. All of this information is critical to managing and optimizing your market value. Your network empowers you to come and go on your terms.

- <u>sharpens your influencing skills</u>. The communication and relationship skills you develop as you build your network will serve you well throughout your career. Just as speeches, debates and interviews with media hone the influencing skills of politicians, the networking process hones your influencing effectiveness. Through networking, you learn how to market and promote yourself, meet new people, and listen.

That being said, most people feel uncomfortable networking and avoid it like the plague[*]. The following comments reflect some of the more common biases: "I hate promoting myself... It feels dishonest and insincere... I am not good at small talk... I don't like to be seen as asking for handouts... It's a waste of time... No tangible results... Shy people can't network... Outgoing people are great at networking. My work speaks for itself."

The key to successful networking is approaching it with Connecting Style in mind – yours and the style of the person with whom you are networking. The Connecting Style Model can help you to identify your natural networking strengths, weaknesses, and strategies that are most effective for you. Knowing the Connecting Style of the person with whom you want to network will help you tailor your approach to build a stronger, more satisfying connection with them. (Refer to Unit 10, Guidelines for Connecting with Each Style.)

The next few pages contain valuable networking advice gleaned from workshops in which each style group discussed their networking experiences and the lessons they learned.

First, let's meet four individuals each representing a Connecting Style at the welcoming cocktail hour at a pharmaceutical industry offsite. Charlie (**Analytical**) is a model networker and yet he is

---

[*] Ironically, some of the most talented students never develop strong networking skills because job opportunities and advancement come easily as they start their careers. At mid-career, they risk ceiling out if they have not learned how to develop a network.

100

hardly a schmoozer. Charlie discussed the industry's latest technology innovations with one person over the course of the hour, whereas Carl (**Energizer**), also a strong networker, engaged a dozen colleagues with his interesting and often entertaining stories. Although June (**Supportive**) interacted with more people than did Charlie but far fewer than Carl, she ended the evening knowing a lot more about others (owing to her excellent listening skills) than they knew about the important work she has been doing (owing to her modesty). Debbie (**Driver**), who showed up late because she was finishing a critical conference call with her team back at the office, interacted with a number of people. Unlike Carl, Debbie did not seek out others as much as others initiated contact with her. Preoccupied with reports waiting to be reviewed back at her hotel room, Debbie left at the earliest opportunity having felt she wasted valuable time.

# Analyticals

**Strengths**: Charlie, like many **Analyticals**, builds highly effective networks around his interests. **Analyticals** are likely to be very active in their churches, communities, politics, and professional associations where they form deep friendships with people who share their interests. Charlie is the president of his state chemical engineering association, a school board member, a member of a traveling brass band, and active contributor to a number of community and political committees. At work, he is typically on a number of task forces in and out of his department. Those relationships, while task and interest centered, are enduring and deeply rooted in mutual respect, a common set of values, and a shared experience of accomplishment and contribution.

In task-focused settings like those mentioned above, many of the personal qualities that characterize these less forcefully assertive styles blossom, contributing to their networking success. They step up as fine, confident leaders and mentors when dealing in subjects they understand and take an interest in. Finally, the reliability and long-term commitment characteristic of **Analyticals** contribute to building trust that makes others comfortable sharing even the most sensitive information with them.

**Challenges:** **Analyticals** find networking is a challenge when it moves away from building relationships around mutual interests to building relationships to serve their own interests, such as networking with the intent of finding a job or selling a product or service. For **Analyticals**, it goes against their independence and professional pride to ask for help – they would much prefer to help others. In addition, **Analyticals'** strong sense of fair play makes them feel like networking to advance one's career is a form of cheating and degrades their professional standards.

# Supportives

**Strengths:** The advantage for **Supportives** when it comes to building a network comes from building on their strengths as team players. They are natural relationship builders and perhaps the most engaging and engagable type. Therefore, like **Analyticals**, joining organizations, associations, and committees representing causes or subjects that matter to them is a great road to building a strong network. As members, they slowly build strong relationships based on the contributions they make and the support they provide. They volunteer generously, can be excellent listeners and great team players in supporting roles, and have little trouble fitting in. The overall impact is quite positive in supporting others' needs to feel understood, included, respected, and valued. **Supportives** can build the kind of networks that give them tremendous access based on the mutual trust and loyalty they typically cultivate with others.

**Challenges:** The hard part is breaking through the resistance of joining new organizations to begin with, and who can blame them? Unlike **Analyticals**, who are often quite confident in the technical expertise and abilities they offer committees and organizations, **Supportives** can be much less self-confident. **Supportives** place more importance on how supportive and welcoming an organization is than **Analyticals**. Either way, joining alone is intimidating. So why not join with friends or colleagues?

More than any other style, **Supportives** are extremely uncomfortable with the self-promotional aspect of networking. They prefer to support and help others and avoid the spotlight. That being said, networking provides a great opportunity for **Supportives** to get more comfortable supporting themselves. Through networking, they get to practice the arts of requesting help, marketing their accomplishments, meeting new people, and otherwise establishing a professional presence among colleagues – all examples of assertiveness that will bolster their effectiveness in their personal lives as well.

# Energizers

**Strengths:** **Energizers** fit the image of what most people imagine when they think of a great networker. They are quite gregarious and welcome the opportunity to meet and socialize with all types of people in all types of situations – people they have never met or old friends. They approach social situations with confidence and warmth and know how to fit in and put others at ease. They are natural promoters and spend a good deal of time sharing and selling their ideas. Like Charlie, Carl volunteers on many committees, attends conferences, and is active in his community.

**Challenges:** **Energizers** make a strong impression – usually a very positive one. However, if they do not balance their talking with listening and awareness of the *Connecting Style* of others, they risk making an unforgettable negative impression. A strong network is built up over time and requires a level of consistency, commitment and dependability that are not strengths for many **Energizers**. They can be very passionate, connected and committed one day and move on to something else more exciting the next. They have a very strong need to feel understood, valued, included, and respected and can be quite sensitive to rejection. Therefore, relationships can sour more easily based on perceived slights. Although **Energizers** appear socially bold, it is not uncommon for them to build networks almost exclusively around non-threatening people – those who they feel look up to them, while avoiding those who they consider a threat.

# Drivers

**Strengths:** When they do meet people, **Drivers**, like Debbie, make a very favorable impression. Unlike **Energizers**, **Drivers**

don't worry too much about pleasing people, so tend to be very direct, to the point, and confident. They build instant credibility as they come across as extremely results oriented and competent – just the kind of strong performer with whom colleagues want to be associated. Their potential as network builders is limited only by their motivation to invest time and energy.

**Challenges:** As much as **Drivers** can build strong networks, very often they don't, especially outside the world they live in everyday. They tend to be so overbooked (since the organizations they work for become very dependent upon them), that they don't have time for networking. **Drivers** will pursue networking to the extent that they can see a direct and tangible benefit to the success of their organization or the work they do.

Like **Analyticals**, the fierce independence of many **Drivers** makes them uncomfortable asking for help from others as when they are looking for a job. Once they recognize how critical networking is to a successful outcome, they discipline themselves and go about building a network. Once they find a job, or no longer see an immediate need to network, their networking activities can drop off precipitously. As with **Energizers**, **Drivers** need to learn that networking depends on long-term and consistent contact with their network. Over time, the lack of a strong network can hurt them in that it limits not only their field of vision of their industries, but their own marketability.

# Recommendations applicable to all four styles:

1. Build on your strengths by being active in as many organizations that represent your interests as you can. Select an association and join it.

2. Enroll in a public speaking workshop or training program as soon as you can. These experiences are perfect for people from all four *Connecting Styles*. They seem to be quite effective in building influencing skills and bolstering confidence in a structured, safe, and enjoyable setting. The organized and goal-oriented approach, the opportunity to see that most people are as uncomfortable as you are in selling themselves, the feedback, and

the highly participative nature of these programs contribute to making it a very positive experience. The hard part is getting yourself to sign up.

3.  Building a network is a direct function of paying attention to and responding to The Six Basic Connecting Needs. Review the behaviors in Unit 3, pages 16-18. Notice how applicable all those behaviors are to building a strong network.

4.  Block out 1 hour per week on your calendar and devote this time to building and refreshing your network.

# Unit 19.
## Stress Resilience

Two of the big differences between school and work are the kind of pressures you will be facing in the workplace and the importance of emotional control and resilience to your success. As an entry-level employee, your resilience will almost certainly be tested. Whether you're a first-year law associate, a marine in basic training, a rookie in the NFL, or a management trainee at a public accounting firm – the drill is the same. You'll be tested to see whether you have what it takes. You might be subjected to long hours, low pay, tedium, or even a lack of respect, but in all cases, your challenge is to keep these pressures from stressing you out.

If you think of stress as the difference between expectations and reality, it makes sense that managing your expectations is a great way to keep from getting stressed out. The more you know about what you're likely to experience, the better off you'll be. The following are some of the more commonplace frustrations, humiliations, and denigrations you can expect as a new employee. Circle the ones that are most likely to push your buttons.

- Being asked to do work that you consider beneath you
- Seeing supervisors or peers bending or breaking rules without consequences
- Having work you are proud of casually dismissed
- Discovering that your supervisor assigned your task to someone else as well
- Discovering you made a mistake
- Dealing with two supervisors who direct you to be in different places simultaneously
- Having to present your work to an audience
- Having to sell an idea to an unknown or unreceptive audience
- Making a request of your supervisor
- Asking your supervisor for clarification

- Being criticized
- Being rejected
- Being confronted
- Being bossed around
- Being manipulated
- Dealing with people who can't make up their mind
- Being talked down to
- Being treated like a child
- Being micromanaged
- Having to stand up for yourself
- Dealing with unreliable people
- Being excluded or dealing with cliques
- Seeing people get recognition you believe is undeserved
- Peers brown-nosing their way to the top

Any of these stressors have the potential to make you feel threatened and activate your survival response – commonly referred to as fight-flight, which means exactly what it sounds like. When confronted with danger, you will either stand and fight or beat a hasty retreat to safety. Once useful to protect us from hungry saber-tooth tigers, this outdated survival mechanism shuts down the most evolved regions of the brain where relationship and communication skills reside and activates the most primitive regions. Unable to distinguish between psychological and physical threat, we overreact to stress across the board and find that our rational thinking has been EMOTIONALLY HIJACKED.

**Fight-flight is:**

1. Automatic and constantly adjusting in response to <u>perceived</u> threats.

2. Physical
   - Cardiovascular
   - Neurological
   - Muscular
   - Digestive
   - Dermatological

3. Emotional
   - Hurt
   - Defensive
   - Impulsive
   - Angry
   - Scared

4. Mental
   - Singular focus on the threat blocks capacity to process important information
   - Difficulty interpreting others' behaviors and intentions
   - Impaired judgment
   - Inflexibility

# Fight-Flight Impact on Behavior by *Connecting Style*

The distinguishing characteristics of each style intensify under stress, and as the judgment centers become dulled and our resources feed the fight-flight engines, the behaviors we count on as assets can become liabilities.

| | |
|---|---|
| **Analyticals/Critical Thinkers**<br>(Avoiding > Controlling<br>>Acquiescing > Attacking)*<br><br>• Remove themselves emotionally<br>• Become difficult to engage | **Drivers/Directors**<br>(Controlling > Avoiding<br>> Attacking > Acquiescing)<br><br>• Take over<br>• Bulldoze |
| **Supportives/Team Players**<br>(Acquiescing > Attacking<br>> Avoiding > Controlling)<br><br>• Over-cooperate to minimize tension<br>• Have trouble asking for what they need | **Energizers/Team Leaders**<br>(Attacking > Acquiescing ><br>Controlling > Avoiding)<br><br>• Attack<br>• Blame and criticize |

---

* Each style has a different initial response to stress. Over time, if the stressor is not resolved, a second response comes into play, then a third and, while quite rare, an individual will eventually react in a fourth way – one that represents the most common stress response of their opposite style. Analyticals act like Energizers; Drivers act like Supportives and vice versa.

# Getting Yourself Out of Fight-Flight

When you feel on the verge of going into fight-flight, regain your balance:

Do not react until you calm down. Bad things happen to good people when they react immediately after being challenged, attacked or insulted. The more wronged you feel, the more important it is to drain your brain of fight-flight hormones before taking action. Your emotionally hijacked brain will urge you to disconnect from your vulnerable feelings by fighting back or withdrawing. Your pride shoves your best judgment aside and wants to run things, making you likely to say things that seem appropriate at the time, but may prove regrettable. Even if you can find the right words, when in fight-flight your body language is likely to broadcast your emotions and cause confusion and defensiveness. An angry or defensive tone can have a powerful and lasting negative impact on the other people in the room and undermine your credibility and ability to influence.

Deactivate fight-flight with deep breathing or any relaxation or meditation technique that works for you:

Begin to focus all of your attention on your breathing. If you open your mouth slightly, you will notice a cool sensation on your lips, which will relax you, and be a good focal point.

As you inhale, locate and stay aware of your physical fight-flight symptoms – e.g., the knot in your stomach, dry mouth, and tight lower back. As you exhale, breathe the discomfort out. Staying connected with the vulnerable feelings and embracing the negative experience as a learning moment KEEPS YOU FROM ACTING, OPENS THE DOOR FOR INCREASING SELF-AWARENESS, AND MAKES YOU MORE RECEPTIVE TO WORKING THE ISSUES OUT. More often than not, you will discover a different, more balanced perspective on the stressful situation, leading the way to a more constructive approach.

**IT'S NOT PERSONAL: Let go of insisting** that other people treat you the way you think you deserve to be treated. The way people behave toward you says more about them than you.

## Getting Someone Else Out of Fight-Flight

When you are interacting with someone who is in fight-flight, it is pointless and self-defeating to argue, explain, debate or tell them to calm down.  The only productive response is to help them get out of the fight-flight spiral.  Here's how:

- Listen, listen and listen.  (non-judgmentally with acceptance)

- Restate what you hear.  ("So what I hear you saying is…")

- Reflect their feelings/emotions.  ("I hear how frustrating this is for you…")

- Ask clarifying questions designed to get them to express their emotions in words.  ("Would it be ok if I ask a question? What exactly is so frustrating about this?")

- Try to figure out which of their needs have been violated. This will help you to figure out how to deal with them. ("Hmmm…it sounds like she was not consulted before the decision was made and probably feels excluded…")

Once the person calms down, you can move on to addressing the problem or issue at hand.


## Managing fight-flight in group settings

One of the first management roles you will experience is leading a meeting, a discussion or presenting to a group of colleagues.  You are now responsible for facilitating the discussion and to some degree managing other people's behavior.  This is a role that forces you to assert yourself and risk hurting others feelings (Drivers and Energizers beware), or not asserting yourself and risk being and feeling taken advantage of (Analyticals and Supportives beware). In addition to applying the behaviors that support the Six Basic Connecting Needs there are some "stress tested" phrases that you can use to address some of the common challenges you will face when presenting. Being prepared with the right words can make a big difference in your confidence and effectiveness. Practice these silently or aloud, imagining in detail the scenario that applies. In time, you will get a feel for what works best for you.

| Challenge | Constructive Approach |
|---|---|
| 1. Responding to a chatterbox who won't shut up at your meeting | Stop speaking and say:<br>• "I'd like to have everyone's attention so you all hear what is being discussed."<br>• "It seems like there are a number of conversations going on. So that we get everyone's valuable input can I please ask that we have one conversation at a time? Thank you." |
| 2. Disagreeing with someone | First, make sure you understand the other person's point of view. Then take any of the following approaches:<br>• Say, "Yes, and..." adding your point of view.<br>• "I appreciate your perspective and would like to add ..." adding your point of view.<br>• "I hear what you're saying, but I see it differently..."adding your point of view. |
| 3. Getting someone to stop dominating a conversation at a meeting you are leading | Using a firm tone and moderate voice, say:<br>• "Thank you for all your input; I would like to see what others have to say."<br>• "Thank you for all your input; let's see what others have to say."<br>• "You have a lot to say on this topic John. To make sure others have the chance to voice their opinions, let's give them a chance to speak now."<br>• "To ensure we have everyone's input, I'd like to use the next few minutes to hear from those who have not yet had a chance to |

| | |
|---|---|
| | speak." |
| 4. Drawing out others who have not provided input / feedback or voiced their opinion | While looking around the room, particularly at those who have not yet spoken, say:<br>• "We've heard a lot of great ideas so far, how about hearing from those who have not yet spoken – even if it's to say that you agree or disagree with what's been said so far." |
| 5. Getting an off-topic conversation back on topic | • "To manage our time so we can get through our agenda - I would like to table that topic for a future meeting or suggest that you/we have that conversation offline – which would you like to do?"<br>• "That sounds like a great idea and I want to allow enough time explore it fully, so why don't we add it to the agenda of our next meeting (or discuss it offline)?"<br>• "We seemed to have gotten off on a tangent, so I'm going to bring us back to the agenda.  Did you want to continue that conversation offline or add it to the agenda of our next meeting (or explore it further and report back to the group in out next meeting or...)?" |
| 6. Handling someone who constantly interrupts the conversation | Using a firm tone and moderate voice, say:<br>• "So we can hear everyone's complete thoughts, can I suggest that when someone is talking, we let them finish their statement, give people a moment to think about what was said, and then |

| | respond?" |
|---|---|
| 7. Getting your voice heard | Sit upright and lean into the conversation; maintain good eye contact; use a firm tone and clearly project your voice when you say, <br>• "I would like to add…" <br>• "I agree, and…" <br>• "Perhaps we should consider…" <br>• "Yes, and…" |

# The Secret to Stress Resilience

Certain people seem to constantly be overwhelmed by stressors while others, facing the same adversity, are able to keep their cool. We call these people stress resilient. What differentiates them are coping skills that serve to: keep things in perspective, reinforce a sense of being in control rather than being controlled as a victim of circumstances, and keep them from taking things too personally. The following section describes the qualities that stress-resilient people have in common.

# Stress Resilience Self-Assessment

The habits and characteristics listed below differentiate those resilient people who are truly able to manage highly stressful work situations from those who get sick, angry, depressed or otherwise stressed out. This exercise allows you to determine how prepared you are for pressure and to identify specific areas to help increase resilience.

**Directions for Scoring**: Rate yourself on how often you demonstrate each of the following stress resilient habits by placing an X in the appropriate box (Often, Sometimes, Rarely). Count the number of X's in each column and enter the total number in line 19. Multiply the number in line 19 by the number in line 20. Enter the result in line 21. Add the three scores together from line 21 and enter the total in line 22. Refer to the key at the bottom to determine your level of stress resilience.

| Stress Resilient Habits | 1 Often | 2 Some times | 3 Rarely |
|---|---|---|---|
| 1. I can accept the things I cannot control. | | | |
| 2. I set my expectations based on reality rather than insist that reality conform to my expectations. | | | |
| 3. I have few rules for how the world should behave. | | | |
| 4. I see obstacles, adversity, and even failure as challenges to overcome and opportunities for growth. | | | |
| 5. I know how to make lemonade out of lemons. | | | |
| 6. I don't take it personally when my basic needs are ignored or violated by others. I do feel hurt, angry, etc., but know how to get past those feelings and solve the real problem. | | | |
| 7. I have a strong network of support and am not afraid to call on that network for help rather than carry burdens alone. | | | |
| 8. Rather than respond as a victim waiting to be rescued, I take action to solve my own problems. | | | |
| 9. I effectively manage my time with good planning and preparing in advance. | | | |
| 10. I try to keep my long-term career goals in mind so that short-term frustration does not bother me so much. | | | |

| Stress Resilient Habits | 1 Often | 2 Some times | 3 Rarely |
|---|---|---|---|
| 11. I accept the fact there will always be detractors. I don't let other people's opinions of me define who I am. | | | |
| 12. I strive for personal excellence, but I can set limits and say no to requests from my boss that I can't fit on my plate. | | | |
| 13. I can assert myself when I feel I am being taken advantage of before I boil over. | | | |
| 14. I can let things go and forgive others and myself. | | | |
| 15. I measure my success more in terms of what I contribute to others than what I get for myself. | | | |
| 16. I maintain a healthy work-life balance. | | | |
| 17. I can live in the here-and-now rather than bemoan the past and worry about the future. | | | |
| 18. I don't take myself too seriously. I can laugh at myself. | | | |
| 19. SUBTOTAL | | | |
| 20. MULTIPLIER | x1 | x2 | x3 |
| 21. SCORE FOR COLUMN | | | |
| 22. TOTAL SCORE | | | |

## KEY:

| Score | Stress Resilience |
|---|---|
| 18-24 | Very Resilient |
| 25-34 | Resilient |
| 35-42 | Borderline Stress Risk |
| 43-54 | Stress Risk |

PART FOUR

# Rules of the Road

# Unit 20.
# The Eight Keys to Early Career Success

The qualities that distinguish outstanding early career success have been organized into the following eight factors or keys:

**I.**   Produce outstanding work with minimal direction

**II.**   Learn and adapt quickly

**III.**   Know yourself

**IV.**   Demonstrate a team first attitude

**V.**   Don't just communicate, connect!

**VI.**   Be resilient

**VII.**   Be accountable for yourself

**VIII.** Express self-confidence (but check your ego at the door)

On the pages that follow, we describe the specific behaviors that comprise each success key. As you read through these factors, keep in mind that:

- They should be adapted to the role/organization you are in
- They will be more or less relevant depending upon your specific role/organization/situations
- You may benefit most from these by identifying a coach or mentor who will act as a sounding board for you as well as help you to apply these ideas

# The Eight Keys to Early Career Success:

## *Development Guide*

| I.  Produce outstanding work with minimal direction |
| --- |

1.  Be disciplined in the way you organize, plan, and prioritize your assignments so you are ready for the demanding, unpredictable, and chaotic times.
    - Quickly learn, adopt and master the calendar/daily appointment and planning system used by your organization.
    - Set aside time at the beginning and end of each workday to review accomplishments, prioritize tasks, and plan next steps.

2.  Make sure you confirm your understanding of your assignments with your supervisor before you begin.  Never guess or assume.
    - Use a project planning tool that lays out what you need to know before starting.
    - Take detailed notes when getting an assignment so you can refer to the specific words later on if the assignment starts to drift or creep.
    - For more complex or ambiguous assignments, take one extra step to think through the assignment and see what questions you still have. Then review it with your supervisor.
    - Email a recap of your meeting and required next steps to your boss so any misunderstandings can be clarified prior to implementation.
    - Ask about other people involved in the task who can be additional resources to you.

3.  Complete assignments on time or ahead of schedule.
    - Do the best you can in negotiating realistic delivery dates at the onset of your assignment to establish a track record for completing assignments on time.
    - Resist the urge to over promise in an effort to make your supervisor happy in the short term.  As a rule of thumb, everything takes 20% longer than you think it will.
    - Anticipate and communicate any delays to your manager and be prepared to suggest alternatives.

4.  Keep your supervisor informed of progress, as well as any unforeseen issues that may cause delays or require changing the original approach. Provide options to work around the obstacles.  Avoid surprises.
    - Agree on the best way to communicate periodic progress:  brief meetings, emails, phone calls, project plan.
    - Keep a record of the challenges that arise over the course of any

assignments so you can review them to identify patterns.

5. Don't reinvent the wheel. Leverage and build on the good work done by others before you. The more you leverage the fine work of people before you, the better your work will be. Many new employees mistakenly believe that relying on others will make them appear weak.

6. Quickly identify and master job-critical tools and technologies such as Microsoft® Excel, PowerPoint, Project, Visio and Word, the company intranet; assorted proprietary research tools; etc.

   • Investigate the corporate intranet (or company's training catalog) for technology tutorials or classes, or take a class at your public library, vocational school, community college, etc.

   • Ask an experienced colleague to show you the key technology tools used during a typical day on the job, and identify people who would make themselves available to answer technology related questions.

   • Learn your company's email and voice mail programs, including how to retrieve messages remotely, out-of-office procedures, and how to access the company address book.

   • Back up your files on a regular basis. Ask about your company's policies for backing up and/or restoring files.

7. Develop your writing skills! The importance of quality writing cannot be overemphasized. Present your ideas effectively and concisely using a style and format appropriate for your audience.

   • Proofread your work before releasing it; check grammar and punctuation – do not rely solely on Spell Check. Keep a dictionary and thesaurus (or bookmark online equivalents) to check spelling and usage.

   • Ask for examples of well-written reports and effective presentations.

   • Ask the strong writers you know to review and edit your written work. Be open to aggressive (and possibly ego-deflating) editing. No pain, no gain.

   • Always write with the recipients' communication style in mind. Consider the level of detail, formality, overall length, etc.

## II.  Learn and adapt quickly

1. Research your industry, market, products, and customers as soon as you can – preferably prior to starting the job.
   - Research the best sources of information (i.e., trade magazines, journals, websites, etc.) to learn more about your industry and market.
   - Learn about your company from information on the corporate intranet or the marketing and communications department.
   - Learn about your company's competitors: know their strengths and weaknesses and how your company compares.

2. Ask your manager to arrange mentoring opportunities.
   - Network with people from related departments (Operations, Marketing, HR, Finance, Technology, Risk, Governance areas, etc.) who can help you learn more about what they do.
   - Be prepared with an outline of what you hope to learn and take careful notes. Be ready to explain your role and responsibilities to them. It is just as important to educate others as it is to learn from them.
   - Ask permission to shadow colleagues whose job functions affect yours. Shadowing is observing someone else's work to get an idea of what they do and how they do it. Plan the experience by creating a task outline and taking notes.
   - Find out who the subject matter experts (SME's) are in your organization. Ask for or create a contact list with their names, areas of expertise, and contact information.

3. Network externally with successful people in your industry through professional associations, alumni groups, and personal contacts.
   - Consider joining a professional organization that offers a mentor program to its members.

4. Pay close attention to behavioral style of the more established and well-regarded members of the organization.
   - Observe behavior in social settings, at the coffee wagon, or the cafeteria.
   - Notice how professional team members dress, behave at meetings, and communicate with management.
   - Be aware of cultural differences – especially if you are working for a non-U.S. company.
   - Distinguish between behaviors deemed acceptable among more established members but not acceptable from those new to the workplace, e.g., *referring to others using nicknames, sharing personal details during a meeting.*

5. Learn your job from the inside out and the outside in.
   - Start with the formal job description, then find out everything you can about the unwritten expectations and rules of the road.
   - Find out who your partners and customers are, their roles, and how they connect with and affect your role. Also, learn how your role impacts others.
   - Shadow others on your team to find out more about your role and how it relates to theirs.
   - Understand and be able to explain the unique value you add to your department and the company. For example, how does your work improve customer satisfaction, product quality, and profits? How does your work contribute to achieving the company's goals, mission, and vision?

6. Know how your performance will be measured and by whom.
   - To avoid surprises, ask your supervisor and colleagues about the performance measurement program and request a copy of the format.
   - Meet with your supervisor to discuss your goals/objectives for the year. Review them regularly to make sure you achieve them.
   - Ask your supervisor for feedback on your performance at regular intervals throughout the year so there are no surprises at the end of the year.
   - Keep a *me* file that includes your development, accomplishments, and accolades (complimentary letters from clients and colleagues). Create a list to discuss with your manager prior to your performance review.

7. Demonstrate openness, curiosity, and a voracious appetite for learning.
   - Exhibit your appetite for learning by making good use of your down time. Take live and online classes, read training manuals, question your manager and colleagues along the way (being respectful of their time).
   - Work with your manager to create and implement a development plan that includes training courses, activities, and tests for understanding along with a timeline that prioritizes the more important learning opportunities.

| III. Know yourself |
| --- |

Know who you are as others see you. Be aware of how you are perceived in different situations with different people. What are the first impressions people typically form of you?

- Review your notes, development objectives, and the Connecting Style sections in this handbook.
- Take a communications skills class that involves self-observation such as a video or tape recording.
- Seek out feedback from trusted co-workers on how you come across, especially in those high-stress situations when emotions run high. Be prepared to take in the feedback, ask for suggestions for developing skills and behaviors, and act on the suggestions.
- Create an action plan to develop areas of weakness.
- Inform your supervisor, mentor and/or trusted colleague about the skills and/or behaviors you are developing and ask for their help or feedback along the way.

---

### IV. Demonstrate a "team first" attitude

---

1. Demonstrate that you put your team's goals and interests before your own.
   - Demonstrate your flexibility and willingness to support change.
   - Volunteer to help other team members by sharing information, giving of your time, showing interest in their work.
   - Express appreciation and give credit to others whenever possible.
   - Refrain from talking about team members behind their backs. When you do have an issue, speak to them directly, one on one.
   - Understand and exhibit your company's values around diversity in the workplace. Respect the opinions and perspectives of others and foster relationships with people who differ from you. Proactively seek out diverse points of view rather than limiting yourself to colleagues who share the same style thinking as you.
   - Do the grunt work on the team if needed. Demonstrate that you are willing to do what is necessary for the team to get the job done.
2. Accept responsibility. Never blame others for your mistakes.
   - Apologize to others when you have offended them or left them out of the loop.
   - If you make a mistake, admit it. If you don't know the answer, say so; don't try to fake it. You will build credibility and trust.

---

### V. Don't just communicate – connect!

---

1. Know how to listen in a way that makes others feel understood, appreciated, and respected.
   - Review the *Listening Habit Self Assessment* and the Tips for Active Listening in this handbook.
   - Take a listening skills class that includes self-observation and feedback.
   - To quiet your mind when listening, practice these four steps: hear, understand, interpret, respond.
   - Focus on understanding the speaker's meaning instead of preparing your response.

2. Master the art of win-win conflict resolution
   - Even when disagreeing, it should be, "Yes, and..."
   - Make clear your desire to find a mutually agreeable solution from the very beginning of a disagreement.
   - The key to conflict resolution is behaving in ways that support the other person's Six Basic Needs – to feel understood, valued, included, respected, autonomous, and to share a level of basic trust. The behaviors described in the Six Basic Needs section are the basis for win-win conflict resolution.

3. Adjust your message to meet the needs of your audience; consider factors including their *Connecting Style*, mood, how important the subject matter is to them, ability to focus at that particular time, and how much time they have.
   - Refer to and utilize the detailed Connecting Style descriptions in this handbook.

4. Excel at the art of asking questions.
   - Ask thoughtful but relevant questions that demonstrate you have been listening.
   - As important as it is to ask good questions, avoid asking questions that show you have not done your homework.
   - Depending on the amount of information you are looking for, use open-ended questions to encourage a more detailed response ("How would you like the report to look?") or closed-ended questions to elicit a one- or two-word answer ("So the report should be limited to two pages, is that right?").

## VI. Be resilient

1.  Know how to keep calm under fire.
    - Overreacting, either in anger or in tears makes a powerful and negative impression.
    - Remember that you can respect other points of view without agreeing. Keep your body language neutral - avoid rolling your eyes, pursing your lips, flaring your nostrils, or any other physical behaviors that might put others on the defensive. Most body language is unconscious, so be aware of your thoughts and emotions and the way in which your body may be communicating non-verbally.
    - Respond without defensiveness when people express contrary views, especially if others are present. Agree to disagree if necessary.

2.  Be able to manage workplace pressures without compromising your physical and emotional well-being.
    - Get involved in activities that are meaningful to you and make you feel energized, both at work and in your personal life – perhaps adopt an enjoyable exercise program to increase your energy level and endurance.
    - Take a lunch break to socialize, laugh and let off some steam, or take a walk around your office building and get some fresh air.

| VII. Be proactive |
|---|
| 1.  Always come prepared!  Bring appropriate materials, documents, and research to meetings.  Review issues in advance.  Think of potential questions/issues.  Take notes.  Follow up.<br>• Prepare for your next meeting by reviewing minutes/notes from the last meeting, looking over the agenda, and thinking about contributions you want to make.<br>• If you will be speaking at the meeting, plan your message beforehand.  Break down your key points and add brief information that supports those points.  Be mindful of the communication styles of your audience.<br>• Provide any materials for review in advance so others have time to prepare.<br>• If you are responsible for the meeting, send out an agenda in advance and follow up with a recap that includes next steps and responsibilities. |
| 2.  Demonstrate energy, enthusiasm, and willingness to take on difficult challenges.<br>• During slow times, ask your manager for additional work.<br>• Show initiative to take on a leadership role and lead a project. |
| 3.  Be able to exercise the discipline and self-control necessary to persevere in the face of extremely frustrating circumstances and obstacles. |
| 4.  When faced with obstacles, take the initiative to approach your work with a 'never-give-up' attitude, even in the face of discouraging conditions or difficult people, rejection or initial failure.<br>• Be persistent but not stubborn.  If your efforts are ineffective, seek feedback and help from your manager or team members.<br>• Observe the conduct of others who appear successful at handling challenging situations.  Ask for their advice.<br>• Learn from past failures and use new approaches. |

| **VIII. Express self-confidence (but check your ego at the door)** |
| --- |

1.  If you are naturally a competitive person:
    - Demonstrate self-confidence by playing support roles, sharing credit, accepting blame, and building others up.
    - Represent yourself and your accomplishments accurately, being careful not to embellish.

2.  If you are naturally a more quietly competitive or cooperative person and are uncomfortable with confrontation and self-promotion:
    - Demonstrate confidence by making your opinions and feelings known, speaking with authority, exhibiting decisiveness, disagreeing when appropriate, and volunteering for leadership roles.
    - Represent yourself and your accomplishments accurately, being careful not to minimize your contribution and value.

3.  Demonstrate optimism and enthusiasm, especially when things are not going well.
    - Refrain from criticizing and complaining about colleagues, customers, or competitors.

You have already had some experience applying many of the behaviors that comprise The 8 Keys to Early Career Success, while others may not yet be relevant to the roles you have played. Before long, all of these behaviors will be instrumental to your success, so it is never too early to start thinking about which ones are relative strengths and which ones will require more attention.

1. Review all 8 Keys and the associated behaviors.

2. Highlight those behaviors that you consider your strengths in green.

3. Highlight those behaviors that you believe come less naturally and will require a focused effort in pink.

4. Prioritize the strengths you highlighted in green and identify two that you can build on by using them more frequently or in different situations.

5. Prioritize the items you highlighted in pink and choose two that you are ready to start working on today.

6. Create a development plan for those two behaviors using the Development Planning Forms in the appendix.

# UNIT 21.
## WORKPLACE ETIQUETTE

| **I. Answering the phone** |
|---|
| ❑ How you come across on the phone is really important. For some people – those geographically distant or with whom you infrequently interact – it contributes significantly to their permanent impression of you. |
| ❑ Find out if your company or department has a standard greeting and use it. |
| ❑ Your greeting should include your company/department name and your first name; it should be enough information to let your caller know they've reached the right place (or not). |
| ❑ Make sure your tone is positive, upbeat, and consistent whether it's your first call of the day or your last. Keeping a small mirror near your phone can remind you to put your 'best face' forward. |
| ❑ Your greeting should be clear; don't rush it! |

| **II. Creating presentations** |
|---|
| ❑ Be prepared with PowerPoint training under your belt. If possible, get experience in a support role for others making presentations. There is no substitute for the expertise you gain as part of the supporting cast. |
| ❑ Learn about the needs and preferences of your audience and design your presentation accordingly. Ask for guidance from the people known for doing great presentations to your audience. You can probably get a copy of other well-received presentations. Ask members of your audience what they are looking for in content and form. |
| ❑ Begin by creating an outline of what key points you want to cover. |
| ❑ Keep the pages easy to read and visually pleasing; don't use a "busy" background, and keep three to five bullets per page. Find out if your company has a standard format or template and use it. |
| ❑ Use the Notes pages in PowerPoint to capture your speaking points for each slide. |
| ❑ Present data in charts and tables. When using images, make sure they are relevant to content on the page. |
| ❑ Have extra copies of your presentation on hand in case additional people attend. |
| ❑ Consider the differences between a presentation on paper and one on the screen. On the screen a dark color background looks great, however they do not usually print well. |
| ❑ Use slide animation and transitions consistently and sparingly. You do not want to detract from your presentation. Avoid using sound effects. |
| ❑ Request feedback after the meeting from your supervisor or coworkers. What could you improve upon? |

| III. Delivering presentations |
|---|
| ❑ You will need to allot substantial time for preparation and rehearsal. |
| ❑ Book conference space well in advance. Make sure your room is big enough to accommodate everyone comfortably. |
| ❑ Visit the room in which your presentation will take place. Familiarize yourself with the set-up, equipment, lighting, and supplies. Note what you'll need to bring. |
| ❑ If you are using technology for your presentation, practice the mechanics and timing so that you can get through it smoothly. |
| ❑ Practice the presentation aloud. Talking points that seem very clear in your mind are not quite as clear when they come out of your mouth. Videotape your practice presentation so you can see and hear how you come across. |
| ❑ Anticipate likely questions. |
| ❑ Before you present, do your best to relax. Visualize what a success you will be. Breathe deeply to calm the nerves. Review and practice the relaxation exercises in this reference guide. |
| ❑ Provide a copy of the presentation in advance to any individuals who are not attending in person. As you speak, let them know what slide you are on. |
| ❑ Avoid memorizing your presentation and/or reading verbatim from the slides. |
| ❑ If asked a question and you don't know the answer, it is best to say so. Offer to get the answer and follow up with the person soon after the presentation. |
| ❑ When presenting to larger groups, make sure you turn your body to address different areas of the room. Maintain good eye contact with all participants – don't forget those who may be on the periphery. Remember to talk to your audience – not into the projection screen or your notes. |
| ❑ Avoid creating distractions during your presentation such as playing with coins or keys in your pocket, clicking the cap on a marker or excessive pacing. |

| IV. Email |
| --- |
| ❑ Identify the style of writing (e.g., formal or conversational) used by your boss, department or company and use it when you create email messages. |
| ❑ Carefully compose and proofread your email as if it were a business letter. Use spell check, look for typos, use proper punctuation and capitalization, and be very careful to spell names properly. You can create a positive or negative impression simply by the way you write. Print out a copy and proofread it carefully. Spell check is not foolproof. |
| ❑ Always carefully check the 'to:' and 'cc:' lines to make sure you are sending to the proper recipient, especially when using 'Reply,' 'Reply All," and 'Forward.' |
| ❑ Remember that emails can easily be forwarded to unintended readers. Make sure that what you are writing is something that would not embarrass you if your boss, colleagues, or someone from another department were to read it. Do not use 'Reply All' if you only need one recipient to read your reply. Few things annoy people more than being inundated with messages they do not need. |
| ❑ Make your 'Subject Line' as meaningful and eye-catching as you can. Since people may receive hundreds of emails each day, you want to make sure yours is one they want to open. |
| ❑ Write your email with your audience in mind. What is the message you want your recipient to receive? Include only essential information about the points you want to make, and cut out any rambling. If you have a timeframe or deadline, make sure that it is clearly stated. |
| ❑ Do not write an email in ALL CAPITALS. IT LOOKS LIKE YOU ARE SHOUTING! |
| ❑ If you are upset or angry, don't put a name in the 'to' field until you are ready to send your email. Instead, save it as a draft, take a break, and read it over again for tone and content. Do you sound defensive or angry? |
| ❑ Emails are archived on your company's server and attached to you for many years. Keep them all business-related and 'politically correct.' |
| ❑ Know that even though you delete an email from the system, most companies can retrieve it from the server. |
| ❑ Avoid using email for personal messages with friends outside the office. Set up/ use a free email account on Hotmail, Yahoo!®, Gmail™, etc. for personal business. |
| ❑ Do not forward confidential information to those who should not see it. It is not uncommon to 'have a conversation' on email and forget there is confidential information at the bottom of the email train. |
| ❑ Know your audience and write accordingly. Be aware of jargon, acronyms, and/or any abbreviations that your audience may not know. If in doubt, spell it out. |
| ❑ When attaching a document/file to the email, make sure you select the right one. Check to make sure any documents you intend to send are |

actually attached.

❑ Don't surf the web at work. It creates the impression you aren't busy. If your projects are temporarily at a standstill, ask if you can help someone else.

❑ Don't use a shared printer to print personal documents or emails.

## V. Voicemail

❑ Learn how to use your company's voicemail system – including the shortcuts that allow you to navigate the system faster. Many systems allow you to re-record your message; if you are rambling, you can use this option to make your message concise and brief.

❑ When leaving a message on another person's voicemail, be brief but leave enough details to move your communication along. Let them know who you are, how to reach you, and what you need from them.

❑ The greeting on your voicemail should mirror the way you answer the phone when you are at your desk. Use the company/department greeting, speak in a positive, upbeat tone and use a steady pace so your callers can understand you.

❑ The greeting on your voicemail should be updated depending on your status in the office. If you are out of the office or in meetings part of the day, include that in your greeting. Let your callers know how they can reach you or an alternate contact, and when you expect to return calls.

❑ Find out how to check your voicemail from outside the office.

❑ Many voicemail systems allow you to use 'urgent' and 'private' options when leaving a message. Use them sparingly and only when needed.

❑ Be careful when forwarding voicemail messages. Make sure you are sending them for the right reasons to the right people.

❑ Some voicemail systems automatically delete old or archived messages every 30 days. Find out what your company's policy is and 're-save' a message if you don't want it deleted.

❑ To avoid missing messages, clean out your voicemail box often. Some voicemail boxes have limited space/room and will not accept any new messages if full.

❑ Don't ignore messages. Reply promptly.

## VI. Meeting etiquette

- ❑ Be sure to arrive on time or early.
- ❑ If you are unable to attend a meeting, notify the team leader in advance and/or send a representative if appropriate.
- ❑ Bring the agenda if it has been sent to you ahead of time.
- ❑ Make sure you take notes, bring your calendar, and follow up on any commitments you make.
- ❑ If you have a topic that you need to discuss, speak to the leader in advance and ask that it be added to the agenda. Provide him/her with the amount of time you need during the meeting.
- ❑ Be prepared to provide others with an update on your assignments.
- ❑ Listen carefully. Ask questions, as appropriate, to clarify your understanding.
- ❑ When someone else is speaking, avoid sidebar conversations with the people next to you.
- ❑ Be aware of specific seating arrangements (e.g., leader at the head of the table).
- ❑ Do not interrupt others. Wait for them to finish, then respond accordingly.
- ❑ Keep confidential information to yourself. Do not be the 'one' to share confidential information around the office.

## VII. Cubicle etiquette

- ❑ Be conscious of keeping your voice at a reasonable level.
- ❑ Do not eavesdrop. If you do overhear things periodically, do not make that obvious to your neighbor and do not gossip to others about what you've heard.
- ❑ Keep your cell phone, pager, or PDA on vibrate during work.
- ❑ Personal photos and effects add a nice touch to your cubicle. Make sure that they are appropriate (no bathing suit photos or shot glasses). Consider the same for any screensavers or wallpaper (on your monitor).
- ❑ Do not loiter outside someone's cubicle – especially if you are with your colleagues and making a lot of noise.
- ❑ If you drop something off in someone's cubicle, do not 'snoop around' their desk and/or read what they may have on their PC monitor.
- ❑ Avoid sneaking up on someone in their cubicle. Make some noise or knock on the wall if you wish to enter. Wait until you are acknowledged and given the okay to enter before you proceed.
- ❑ If you must use your speakerphone in your cubicle (for a meeting with others in your cubicle), be conscientious of your neighbors and keep the volume of the phone and your conversation low. If possible, use a conference room instead.
- ❑ Avoid yelling across cubicles to talk to a colleague. Walk over to your colleague's cubicle or call him on the phone.

- ❑ If you'd prefer to listen to music, first check to see if it's OK, then use headphones to avoid disturbing your neighbors. Don't sing or hum along!
- ❑ Be aware of the scents coming out of your cubicle – keep your shoes on, minimize your use of cologne/perfume, and avoid eating strong aromatic foods at your desk.

## VIII. Setting limits

- ❑ Sometimes you will have to say no (or some version of it) to a project or a deadline. Ask your manager or mentor for guidance to help you prioritize.
- ❑ Do not use vague language. Be clear, polite, firm and offer alternatives: "I am unable to do that, but what I can do is..."
- ❑ Explain that you are unable to do the entire job right now due to other commitments, but ask if there is something specific (one aspect of the request/project) that you can provide for them.
- ❑ Make sure you understand exactly what is being asked of you. The task may be bigger than what you can handle right now or it might just be a small request that you can turn around quickly.
- ❑ Sometimes you have to say yes. If that is the case, you can take the following actions:
- ❑ Tell the person you will do it this time, however you would like to discuss ways to plan better in the future.
- ❑ Tell them yes, but you set the timetable if at all possible... "I will have this done for you next Tuesday by 9:00 a.m."
- ❑ Place a condition on the situation... "I can give you two hours of my time at the end of the day."

## IX. Managing difficult people

- ❑ You can't control or change others, but you can control how you respond to them. Keep a positive attitude and do not meet difficult people on their level. Show them how you would like to be treated. You will be remembered for your attitude in response to another's.
- ❑ If you've had a difficult encounter with someone, look at your next encounter as an opportunity to build a positive relationship. Try a different approach, look for common ground, and use supportive language.
- ❑ Identify what it is about that person that is difficult to deal with.
- ❑ Keeping their style in mind, flex your style to accommodate their needs.
- ❑ If one of their six basic needs has been violated, figure out which need it was and use behaviors that support the need to deal with that individual.
- ❑ Observe others who have a good working relationship with the 'difficult' person. Emulate their behavior when working with the difficult person.
- ❑ No matter how tempting, don't complain about that person to others. It will inevitably get to them and boomerang. If you have an issue with someone, either address it directly or keep your feelings to yourself.

## X. Managing cultural diversity

❏ If your company deals with people from other countries or regions, find out about time zones, currencies, local holidays and customs. Don't always set meeting times that are most convenient for you – flex your schedule to accommodate other time zones.

❏ Examine your own beliefs and attitudes about different cultures, races, and ethnicities.

❏ Consider what it may be like to work in another country or come from another country and work in the U.S.

❏ Be patient when working with someone with a heavy accent from another country. Most people in the U.S. speak English; however, people from other countries are fluent in their own language and other languages including English. Can you speak fluently in other languages?

❏ If the situation is comfortable, ask colleagues and customers to tell you about themselves. Show interest in their families and interests and share appropriate information about yourself. If someone is reluctant to share, respect that and keep the relationship positive.

# UNIT 22.
## CAREER ENTRY CHECKLIST

When you start a new job, you have some unique opportunities. First, you may have more available time when you begin a new job, at least more than you will have once your boss figures out how good you are! Take advantage of that opportunity. Second, you have permission to ask questions; after all, you are new. Use that opportunity to satisfy your curiosity, being sensitive to asking the right questions of the right people. Remember, there are many sources of information available to you in addition to asking questions.

This list is intended to get you started thinking about how to enter a new organization and what sorts of information, skills, and behaviors can get you through the learning curve, integrated into the organization, and productive as fast as possible. If some of these items seem quite obvious, give yourself permission to roll your eyes. However, we would rather list five things you already considered if it means listing one that might not have occurred to you!

Reminder: Review the *Eight Keys to Early Career Success* in Unit 20. Refresh your understanding of your *Connecting Style*, the other styles, and the *Connecting Styles and Tips* in Unit 8.

## Your Attitude

❑ Remember that everything you do or say counts.

❑ Make a good impression, beginning with the first day.

❑ Make an effort (even if you are shy) to meet as many people as you can – on your team and on your floor. Keep track of names, titles, and job responsibilities.

❑ Be aware of eye contact and confident body language. Give verbal and non-verbal cues that you are following along with conversation and ask questions for clarification.

❑ Demonstrate your optimism and resilience. Do not get caught up in complaining or gossip.

❑ Choose to do your best.

❑ Continuously learn, looking for the opportunity in every situation.

# The Organization

This is your chance, before you dive narrow and deep, to learn in broad strokes what the organization you just joined is all about! Go for it!

❑ How did the organization begin?

❑ What is the mission of the organization?

❑ What is the vision of the organization?

❑ What is the physical layout of the facility (plant, building)?

❑ What is the nature of the industry of which your organization is a part?

❑ Where is the organization positioned in its industry?

❑ What are the organization's products and/or services?

❑ Who are the key players in the organization? (CEO, department heads, your boss, your boss' boss).

❑ How are products manufactured or services delivered? Prepare a workflow.

❑ Who are the customers? How does the organization differentiate their products to keep customers happy?

❑ Who are the competitors? How do your products/services compare to theirs?

❑ How do the various departments interact to achieve the organization's goals?

❑ What are the organization's key policies, procedures, and rules? Include HR policies, risk policies, and procedures.

❑ Understand what your company's values are around diversity, community involvement, corporate citizenship, and employee behaviors that would support them.

## Your Relationship with the Organization

Doubtless someone will be orienting you to the specifics of your job, but be sure to explore your full relationship with the organization.

❑ What is your job specifically and how does your job impact others? Where are you in the workflow?

❑ Who are the people on your team? From whom do you receive work/instructions? To whom do you give work/finished product? What are the quality standards by which your work is measured?

❑ Who are the people around you to whom you can ask questions?

❑ What insurance and educational benefits are available to employees?

❑ How do sick leave and vacation leave accrue and when are you eligible to receive/use them? How is time off scheduled and how far in advance?

❑ What are your boss' expectations of you?

❑ What role will he/she play? (i.e., mentor, customer, resource provider)

❑ How does he/she prefer to be communicated with and what is his/her Connecting Style?

## Tools

It sounds simple, but most of us completely underutilize the tools we have available. Now is your time to learn to use them to their fullest.

❏ Practice using the tools of your trade, including email, the relevant software, and the phone system. Put a mental filter on before you send an email – your work emails should not sound like personal emails.

❏ Practice accessing the various forms or tools you will be required to use (time sheets, vacation planners, and procedural documents).

❏ Adopt a daily organizing system and make daily organizing a habit, incorporating weekly planning and monthly benchmarks that tie into your annual objectives.

❏ Take time to navigate through the company website thoroughly. There is a wealth of information there. Research articles about your company, explore HR policies, read executive biographies, and look for training opportunities.

## Activities

Suggested activities you may be able to arrange for yourself if they are not provided.

❏ Explore and sign up for any training or development activities that target new hires.

❏ Request a tour of the building/facility. Introduce yourself along the way. Include any departments with which you will be interacting. No tour? Explore on your own!

❏ Set up lunches with key people (your boss, co-workers, HR rep, etc.).

❏ Request relevant written information: organization charts, presentations, websites, policies, procedures, marketing brochures.

143

❑ Use your daily organizer, diary, or PDA and set aside time at the beginning and end of each workday to prioritize tasks, examine accomplishments, and plan next steps. This is a good habit to establish and will help you succeed when the workload becomes heavy.

❑ Request a copy of personnel policies, risk policies, codes of conduct, etc.

❑ Make note of fire and security procedures and exits.

❑ Interview people. Prepare a short set of relevant questions such as: What does this person do? How is his/her area related to mine?

❑ Identify the top 5-10 resources (websites, trade publications, associations, etc.) for learning information about your company, industry, market, product, customer, etc.

❑ Ask for or find a mentor. Using a mentor can help you accelerate your learning, expand your network, develop your skills/behaviors, and enhance your career.

# UNIT 23.
## COMMON CAREER DERAILERS

*The following are some of the career-damaging behaviors that you should be most aware of according to the managers interviewed in our survey:*

1. Angry outbursts, pouting, humiliating someone, losing control, swearing and inappropriate joking

*"Don't make jokes. Don't put anyone down." "Let the senior members tell the jokes and take the social lead."*
*"Don't swear! I have had to fire people for saying stupid things— foul language."*

2. Excessive Partying – Don't be that guy or gal

*"Don't be the life of the party or too eager to go out for a drink. It never looks good."*
*"Going out for drinks – you have to do it – when in Rome. But never get drunk. Stay strategic. If the client or boss gets rowdy, don't follow. But you can learn an awful lot...like an undercover agent. Listen but don't get involved in the mix."*

3. Circumventing authority and not keeping the right people in the loop

*"Understand the rules about chain of command. Be careful of reaching up above your boss. Your boss is your key supporter, no matter what. Make sure he feels respected and included. You have no political or personal agenda. Make yourself his/her project."*

4. Arrogance

*"If you have the need to dominate and sound smart – know it all – you set yourself up for failure."*
*"You will be all juiced up and feeling as smart as Warren Buffet, but you basically know nothing when you arrive. It is a real turn off when young people show off what they know."*
*"Nobody cares how smart you are. It has very little to do with that. Do you want to be the super smart guy others hire or the one who hires others?"*

*"Don't overvalue the knowledge you bring to the job."*

5. Dishonesty

*"Always tell the truth! Whether it's inflated expense reports, excessive time off, representing your accomplishments, accepting gifts, taking credit for others' work, you will always find examples of senior people who cross the line. Follow at your own risk. Read the company's ethics and HR policies."*

6. Improper use of email and/or voicemail

*"Use email and voicemail for business only. Do not send inappropriate messages to anyone in the organization – especially since they can get forwarded to the wrong person and get you fired."*

# UNIT 24.
## CAREER RISK FACTOR SELF-ASSESSMENT

Instructions: Read each risk factor and put a ✓ in the box that best describes the likelihood of each factor being a risk for you. Discuss your self-perceptions with a mentor, coach or other person who knows you well and is likely to give you honest feedback.

| Risk Factors | Highly Likely | Possible but not Likely | Very Unlikely |
|---|---|---|---|
| Too modest | ☐ | ☐ | ☐ |
| Arrogant | ☐ | ☐ | ☐ |
| Too accommodating and nice | ☐ | ☐ | ☐ |
| Excessive partying in business social settings | ☐ | ☐ | ☐ |
| Keeping feelings, opinions, and convictions to self | ☐ | ☐ | ☐ |
| Indecisive | ☐ | ☐ | ☐ |
| Overbearing | ☐ | ☐ | ☐ |
| Cynical | ☐ | ☐ | ☐ |
| Visibly defensive and/or angry | ☐ | ☐ | ☐ |
| Circumventing authority; not keeping the right people in the loop | ☐ | ☐ | ☐ |
| Not volunteering for stretch roles | ☐ | ☐ | ☐ |
| Earning a reputation as someone who is never on time | ☐ | ☐ | ☐ |
| Procrastinating | ☐ | ☐ | ☐ |
| Inappropriate use of email and/or voicemail | ☐ | ☐ | ☐ |

# Appendix

# DEVELOPMENT PLANNING FORMS

**Directions for creating development plans:**

1. Write your development goal. Be specific.

2. Write down two action steps that will help you achieve your goal.

3. Identify potential obstacles to change and the strategies for working through them.

## Sample Development Plan

| | |
|---|---|
| **Development Goal:** | |
| Let people finish their sentences before I respond. In other words, stop cutting them off when they are talking. | |

**Action steps:**

1. Count to three after they finish their comments before responding.

2. Ask my colleagues to help me become more aware of the times I cut people off by providing me with feedback when I do – and don't – cut people off or finish their sentences.

| Obstacles | Strategies |
|---|---|
| • Stress on the job – everything is a crisis and I just have to react.<br>• I'm used to behaving this way.<br>• At the time, I feel justified in interrupting, and only later realize it was not so important that it could not have waited. | • Change my mindset. Think differently. Be conscious of how I make other people feel when I cut them off.<br>• Place a Post-it Note near my phone that reminds me to let people finish their sentences.<br>• Ask my partner to give me a sign when I cut people off.<br>• Make the effort to change. It will be awkward at first, but the outcome will be worthwhile. |

**Development Goal #1**

**Action steps:**

1. _____

   _____

   _____

2. _____

   _____

   _____

| Obstacles/Challenges | Strategies |
|---|---|
|  |  |

**Notes:**

_____

_____

_____

_____

_____

_____

**Development Goal #2**

**Action steps:**
1. _____
   _____
   _____
2. _____
   _____
   _____

| Obstacles/Challenges | Strategies |
|---|---|
|  |  |

**Notes:**
_____
_____
_____
_____
_____
_____

**Development Goal #3**

**Action steps:**

1. _____

_____

2. _____

_____

_____

| Obstacles/Challenges | Strategies |
|---|---|
| | |

**Notes:**

_____
_____
_____
_____
_____
_____

**Development Goal #4**

**Action steps:**
1. _____
   _____
   _____
2. _____
   _____
   _____

| Obstacles/Challenges | Strategies |
|---|---|
|  |  |

**Notes:**
_____
_____
_____
_____
_____
_____

**Development Goal #5**

**Action steps:**
1. _____
   _____
   _____
2. _____
   _____
   _____

| Obstacles/Challenges | Strategies |
| --- | --- |
| | |

**Notes:**
_____
_____
_____
_____
_____
_____

**Development Goal #6**

**Action steps:**

1. _____
   _____
   _____

2. _____
   _____
   _____

| Obstacles/Challenges | Strategies |
|---|---|
|  |  |

**Notes:**
_____
_____
_____
_____
_____
_____

**Development Goal #7**

**Action steps:**

1. _____

_____

_____

2. _____

_____

_____

| Obstacles/Challenges | Strategies |
|---|---|
|  |  |

**Notes:**

_____

_____

_____

_____

_____

_____

**Development Goal #8**

**Action steps:**

1. _____

_____

_____

2. _____

_____

_____

| Obstacles/Challenges | Strategies |
|---|---|
| | |

**Notes:**

_____

_____

_____

_____

_____

_____

# Early Career Success Research

**From Barbara Kovach, *Organizational Dynamics* "The Derailment of Fast Track Managers" ( Rutgers University, 1986)**

"Many young managers are launched on the fast track only to be derailed at the higher levels of mid-management when they fail to meet a new set of expectations."

"For high energy, self-directed, technically strong individuals with an eye toward getting results, promotions and raises can come fast and furious in the early phases of their careers."

"A great many of these strong individual contributors will either derail or ceiling out in mid career as they become eligible for roles with increasing emphasis on people handling, because they never developed critical teamwork and influencing skills."

"They almost always report feeling blindsided when they hit that ceiling and discover the gap between their positive intentions and their actual negative impact of their behavior on others. It is easy to fall into a false sense of self-satisfaction about one's effectiveness. The rewards young people receive in their early years of their careers tend to be interpreted as validation for every aspect of their performance, when in fact, many of the behaviors that would ultimately derail them were apparent, but didn't really come into play because their role was primarily that of individual contributor."

Early career: high-energy, initiative, self-assertion.

New expectations in mid-career: "Acquire the essential personal power to influence and motivate large groups of people. To create an environment that encourages employees to perform at high levels."

**From Reed Larson in *American Psychologist,* "Toward a Psychology of Positive Youth Development (January 2000, pages 170 – 183)**

"In the emerging heterogeneous global society where job demands and basic life course and life style decisions are not pre-configured, adolescents will need to acquire the motivation and skills to create order, meaning, and action out of a field of ill structured choices. Individuals will need the capacity to exert cumulative effort over time to reinvent themselves, reshape their environments, and engage in other planful undertakings. A generation of bored and challenge avoidant young adults is not going to be prepared to deal with the mounting complexity of life and take on the emerging challenges of the 21st century."

**From US News and World Report (April 9, 2007)**

"Indeed, a growing number of employers agree that it is communication, leadership, teamwork, and other so-called soft skills that truly distinguish MBA candidates today. According to a 2006 survey by the Graduate Management Admission Council, nearly two fifths of employers say these are extremely important in selection and hiring."

Business schools are responding with offerings on topics like ethics, negotiation and persuasion, business writing, and, yes occasionally even the arts. Some are launching entire programs dedicated to soft skills. Starting next year, for example, all first-year students at Vanderbilt's Owen Graduate School of management will participate in Learning to Lead, which will include personality assessments as well as executive coaching and voluntary activities such as military leadership simulations. At the University of Texas-Austin McCombs School of Business, all first-year students now pay $800 for the first two semesters of the extracurricular Plus program, which includes services like Coach-on-Call for help preparing a presentation or advice about presentations and job-skills seminars.

162

Teamwork, of course, is now part of nearly every MBA curriculum. At the Tuck School of Business at Dartmouth College, for example, students work in groups in 75 percent of their classes, and half of all grades are issued to teams. Students get constant anonymous feedback from their peers; they also design individual leadership development plans, which track strengths, weaknesses, progress, and goals and are similar to the personal development portfolios required at institutions like Northeastern University. "Some people say leaders are born, not made, but we don't believe that," says Tuck Dean Paul Danos. "We think we can push students up the ladder of leadership faster by exposing them to as many different experiences as possible and making them sensitive to their own skills and how they're coming across."

For those who think classes in leadership and communication sound like fluff, administrators warn that soft skills are actually hard work. "They involve our own emotions and other people in a way that technical skills do not," says Bruce Clark, the faculty coordinator for the MBA program at Northeastern.

**From "Management Education at Risk," Report of the Management Education Task Force to the Association to Advance Collegiate Schools of Business (AACSB) International Board of Directors, (August, 2002)**

"Collected evidence from business school alumni suggests that the most important predictor of business success is management effectiveness. Alumni rate interpersonal, leadership, and communication skills as highly important in the business world, yet they often rate these skills as among the least effective components of business school curricula. For example, in a recent study of U.S. programs by AACSB and Educational Benchmarking, Inc., alumni of both full- and part-time MBA programs ranked one-to-one interpersonal skills highest in importance. However, less than 6 percent of the programs evaluated earned an effectiveness rating higher than 5.5 on a seven-point scale."

The Graduate Management Admission Council Global MBA Survey, in which graduates are asked to assess their personal effectiveness in a variety of areas, suggests that U.S. programs may be stronger in teaching interpersonal, leadership, and communication skills than non-U.S. programs. Relative to the self-reports of students in other countries, alumni of U.S. programs who answer the survey generally say their business programs helped them make stronger improvements in these areas.

**From USA Today, June 10, 2004, quoting Bill Coplin, Professor of Public Policy at the Maxwell School and the College of Arts and Sciences, Syracuse University, and author of 10 Things Employers Want You to Learn in College.**

"Surveys of employers put work ethic, communications, information-gathering and people skills at the top of the list, followed by analytical and problem-solving skills. These capabilities apply across all fields. Despite the consensus on the importance of these professional abilities, many college graduates lack them, according to a 1999 report by the Business Higher-Education Forum and studies of the Collegiate Employment Research Institute at Michigan State University. Corporate recruiting managers confirm that students may have technical skills, but they tend not to have soft skills.

Students in technical fields, such as engineering or the physical sciences, or those destined for graduate programs, such as law or an MBA, need to pay particular attention to communication and group work. Graduate-school recommendations ask more questions about attitude, commitment and people capabilities than intelligence and analytical ability. They may weigh standardized tests most, but soft skills matter."

### From Jim Kelly, Financial Times (London, May 8, 2002)

"The results of a survey for the Financial Times organized by the Association of Graduate Recruiters provide support for efforts to make lifelong learning a big issue for companies. The data showed that employers rated a willingness to train as the second most important key to success for graduates – only outstripped by interpersonal skills. Using college to build a healthy set of professional skills will lead to a good job in a reasonable amount of time and help minimize layoff fears, which, in today's economy, never disappear.

Mr. Gilleard, chief executive of the Association of Graduate Recruiters, said the high value given to interpersonal skills showed that in almost all industries there were no longer niches for people who could not communicate or work in a team."

### From Christine Lee in Asian Diversity Magazine, "Graduating Colleges, But Not To Leadership Positions," ( 2005)

"Despite their high enrollment in U.S. colleges and universities, few Asian Americans are making the leap into corporate America's small nebula of managerial positions.

So why are Asian Americans being shut out from the corner office, even though they are one of the most highly educated minorities in the nation? Answers range from cultural and language barriers to the stereotypes that Asian Americans may still face.

'There's a tendency to value Asian Americans for technical ability, but also a stereotype that we don't make good leaders,' said Paul Igasaki, vice chair of the U.S. Equal Employment Opportunity Commission (EEOC).

Igasaki maintains that Asian Americans must take responsibility for their advancement in corporate America as well.

'Because many Asian Americans may have an accent, they may feel self-conscious about speaking up in group settings. In addition, some Asian Americans do not understand the importance of socializing and networking to corporate advancement,' Igasaki said.

'We need to look at our own actions to make sure we are taking all our opportunities,' he said."

On the other hand, many of the qualities that define the millennial generation help prepare them for success in a globalized workplace.


**From Morley Winograd and Michael D. Hais in The Washington Post , "The Boomers Had Their Day. Make Way for the Millennials" (Sunday, February 3, 2008, page B01)**

"Today's millennials are the largest generation in U.S. history — twice as large as Generation X and numbering a million more than the baby boomers. Though nearly 90 percent of the GI generation was white, it was diverse for its time. Many members were immigrants or the children of Catholic and Jewish immigrants. About 40 percent of millennials are of African American, Latino, Asian or racially mixed backgrounds. Twenty percent have at least one immigrant parent.

Millennials' political style is also similar to the GI generations. They aren't confrontational or combative, the way boomers (whose generational mantra was "Don't trust anyone over 30") have been. Nor does the millennials' rhetoric reflect the cynicism and alienation of Generation X, whose philosophy is, "Life sucks, and then you die." Instead, their political style reflects their generation's constant interaction with hundreds, if not thousands, of "friends" on Myspace or Facebook about any and all subjects, increasingly including politics. Since they started watching "Barney" as toddlers, the millennials have learned to be concerned for the welfare of everyone in the group and to try to find consensus, "win-win" solutions to any problem. The result is a collegial approach that attracts millennials to candidates who seek to unify the country and heal the nation's divisions."


**From David Butcher in Career Development International, "Meta-ability Development: A New Concept for Career Management " (1998 Volume 3, Issue 2, pages 75 – 78)**

Butcher and his colleagues at Cranfield School of Management are leading researchers in understanding the qualities that distinguish the best performers, managers, and leaders the corporate workplace. Their extensive body of research boiled down the qualities necessary to succeed in the global world of politics, personalities, dysfunctional culture and constant change into four "meta-abilities" or foundational success skills.

| Cognitive skills | Self knowledge | Emotional resilience | Personal drive |
|---|---|---|---|
| -Cognitive complexity -Cognitive flexibility -Visionary ability -Gaining clarity -Perceptual acuity | -Self awareness -Awareness of one's own impact on others | -To exert self-control and discipline -To manage emotions appropriately -To be personally resilient in coping with pressure and adversity -To have a balanced view of self | -Ambition for responsibility -Ability to motivate oneself and others -Ability to take personal risks |

**From Amy Cynkar in *Monitor on Psychology, "Outcomes that matter,"* (November 2007, vol. 38, no. 10)**

Based on a survey conducted by The Association of American Colleges and Universities (AAC&U), 63% of over 300 employers surveyed believe that college graduates are not prepared with the practical skills and global awareness they need to succeed. 76% of all employers say colleges and universities should place more emphasis on teamwork skills and the ability to collaborate with others in diverse group settings.

To combat this deficiency, a consortium of college professors created Liberal Education and America's Promise (LEAP). Their research leads to four essential learning outcomes:

1. Knowledge of human cultures and the physical and natural world

2. Extensive training in intellectual and practical skills
3. Personal and social responsibility
4. Integrative learning

**Finally a quote by Nicholas Kristof in *The New York Times*, "Saving the World in Study Hall," (May 11, 2008)**

"In keeping with thousands of years of tradition, I should be wringing my hands about adolescents these days, so lazy and degenerate compared with my own upstanding generation. But when I see high school students working energetically to save the lives of people half a world away, before they are even allowed to buy a beer, I'm reduced to mumbling admiration. These kids are truly inspiring."

# ADDITIONAL RESOURCES – WEBSITES

**America's Career Infonet**

A resource for making informed career decisions, including information about various occupations, industries, and states. Search the Job Bank, find out about job credentials for various fields, or access and use the Employer Locator.

URL: http://americascareerinfonet.com/

**Career Builder**

Use Career Builder's "job-matching technology" that delivers jobs to you that match your interests. The more you use Careerbuilder.com, the better the job matches become.

URL: http://www.careerbuilder.com/

**CareerJournal**

Executive career site that brings you the exceptional resources of the *Wall Street Journal*. Thousands of career-related articles from the *Wall Street Journal*, job search database with over 100,000 opportunities, interview preparation tools, resume support, discussions. CareerJournal's unlimited JobSeek Agents will alert candidates whenever a job is added that matches their criteria.

URL: http://www.careerjournal.com/

**Career Success for Newbies**

Provides first-time job seekers with tools, tips and a guide for a successful career, work and life. Topics include: personal goal-setting, breaking bad habits, time management, stress in the workplace and other practical advice.

URL: http://career-success-for-newbies.com/

## Employment Guide

Take a free career test. Search for jobs by state. Have job alerts sent to you.
URL: http://www.employmentguide.com

## Hot Jobs (by Yahoo)

Access and save your job searches, create and save versions of your resume and cover letters, leverage career tools such as networking tips.
URL: http://hotjobs.yahoo.com/

## Job

Gear for your career.
URL: http://www.job.com

## Job Employment Guide

Like someone said, "The old career was a marriage. The new career is a date." This website gives you a complete, up-to-date and comprehensive job search and employment guide, covering career planning, resume writing, job search, interview skills, salary negotiation, resignation, self-employment, etc.
URL: http://www.job-employment-guide.com

## Job Finder USA

We offer an easy to use employment website geared towards you. Access a free account where you can store resumes and cover letters and apply for jobs with ease.
URL: http://www.jobfinderusa.com

## Job Hunt

Online job search guide—help and links to 9,800 resources and employers. "Best" site for job hunting and careers according to *Forbes* and *PC Magazine* and also a *US News & World Report* "Top site for finding work."

URL: http://www.job-hunt.org

## Monster

The most well known and most-hit career web site. Post your resume, search for jobs, look for job fairs in your area, research degree programs, and seek career advice.
URL: http://www.monster.com/

## Quintessential Careers

A leader in career and job-search advice. Now in its tenth year of operations, and with more than 3,100 pages of free college, career, and job-search content to empower your success in life.
URL: http://www.quintcareers.com/

## The Ladders

The premium job site created exclusively for $100K people looking for $100K jobs. Over 70,000 jobs.
URL: http://www.thcladders.com

## The Riley Guide (receives support from *The Wall Street Journal*)

A directory of employment and career information sources and services on the internet, primarily intended to provide instruction for job seekers on how to use the Internet to their best advantage. Does not contain a job search, but brings the expertise of an experienced librarian and internet search pioneer. This site has been active since 1994, but its articles are current.
URL: http://www.rileyguide.com/

## US Government Jobs

Resources for finding and getting jobs in government. Links to hundreds of federal, state and local job vacancy and information websites
URL: http://www.usgovinfo.about.com/od/governmentjobs

**Vocational Information Center**

Explore vocational and technical careers, check out the skills employers really want, find a trade school, research technical topics and look at the current job market. Search for information about specific careers, workplace skills, technical schools, and market information.

URL: http://www.khake.com/

# ADDITIONAL RESOURCES - BOOKS

Adler, Ronald B. and Jeanne Marquardt Elmhorst. *Communicating at Work – Principles and Practice for Business and the Professions.* New York: McGraw-Hill, 2005. Eighth Edition.

Bolton, Robert. *People Skills: How to Assert Yourself, Listen to Others and Resolve Conflict.* New York: Simon and Schuster, 1986.

Bolton, Robert and Dorothy Grover Bolton. *People Styles at Work.* New York: AMACOM, 1996.

Covey, Stephen R. *The 7 Habits of Highly Effective People.* New York: Fireside Books, 1989.

Gebelein, Susan H., Lisa A. Stevens, Carol J. Skube, David G. Lee, Brian L. Davis, and Lowell W. Hellervik,. *Successful Manager's Handbook.* Minneapolis, Minnesota: Personnel Decisions International Corporation, 2000. Sixth Edition.

Marcum, Dave, Steve Smith, and Mahan Khalsa. *BusinessThink.* New York: John Wiley and Sons, 2002.

Stone, Douglas, Bruce Patton, and Sheila Heen. *Difficult Conversations.* New York: Viking, 1999.

# Steven Lurie, Ph.D.

SLURIE@LEDONLINE.COM

Steven Lurie is a Psychologist with over twenty-five years of experience consulting, coaching, and teaching in a wide range of organizational and educational settings.

Dr. Lurie founded the leadership development firm, Lurie Executive Development (*LEDonline.com*) in 1986, specializing in coaching, team building and collaborative change management. His clients have included companies representing a wide range of industries including financial services, entertainment, consumer products, pharmaceuticals, health care, fashion, public accounting, advertising and manufacturing.

He recently started *Empowered Life Strategies, Inc.* (*empoweredlifestrategies.com*) to provide workshops and training for students and others who have historically not had access to the training and development opportunities normally afforded those in the management ranks of the private sector. His *Connect for Success* workshops are offered extensively at colleges and universities, such as NYU-Stern School of Business and Sarah Lawrence College.

Dr. Lurie is currently Associate Clinical Professor at Adelphi University, Garden City, NY and has held faculty appointments at Yeshiva and St. John's Universities.

He earned a B.A. in Psychology from Brandeis University in 1975, and Ph.D. in Psychology from Adelphi University, Garden City, NY, where he then completed a four-year postdoctoral program in psychoanalysis and psychotherapy.

Dr. Lurie is a member of the American Psychological Association.

# NOTES

[1] Thomas L. Friedman, <u>The</u> *World is Flat: A Brief History of the Twenty-first Century*, (New York: Ferrar, Straus and Giroux, 2005)

[2] Portia Nelson, *There's a Hole in My Sidewalk: The Romance of Self-Discovery*, (Beyond Words Publishing Company, 1994. ISBN: 0941831876)

[3] Dave Marcum, Steve Smith and Mahan Khalsa, *BusinessThink, Rules for Getting It Right – Now and No Matter What*, (New York: John Wiley and Sons, Inc., 2002)

Printed in the United States
146369LV00003BA/4/P